Mindfulness and
Schema Therapy

Mindfulness and Schema Therapy

A Practical Guide

Michiel van Vreeswijk
Jenny Broersen
Ger Schurink

Translation by Jan van der Tempel

WILEY Blackwell

This edition first published 2014
© 2014 John Wiley & Sons, Ltd.

Registered Office
John Wiley & Sons, Ltd, The Atrium, Southern Gate, Chichester, West Sussex, PO19 8SQ, UK

Editorial Offices
350 Main Street, Malden, MA 02148-5020, USA
9600 Garsington Road, Oxford, OX4 2DQ, UK
The Atrium, Southern Gate, Chichester, West Sussex, PO19 8SQ, UK

For details of our global editorial offices, for customer services, and for information about how
to apply for permission to reuse the copyright material in this book please see our website at
www.wiley.com/wiley-blackwell.

The right of Michiel van Vreeswijk, Jenny Broersen and Ger Schurink to be identified as the
author of this work has been asserted in accordance with the UK Copyright, Designs and
Patents Act 1988.

Library of Congress Cataloging-in-Publication Data

Vreeswijk, Michiel van.
  Mindfulness and schema therapy : a practical guide / Michiel van Vreeswijk, Jenny Broersen,
Ger Schurink.
    pages cm
  Includes bibliographical references and index.
  ISBN 978-1-118-75318-7 (cloth) – ISBN 978-1-118-75317-0 (pbk.)   1. Attention.
2. Schema-focused cognitive therapy.   I. Title.
  BF321.V74 2014
  616.89′1425–dc23
                                                       2014005686

A catalogue record for this book is available from the British Library.

Cover image: © Mikadun/Shutterstock
Cover design by Design Deluxe

Set in 10.5/14pt Plantin by SPi Publisher Services, Pondicherry, India
Printed and bound in Malaysia by Vivar Printing Sdn Bhd

1 2014

Contents

Contents

About the Authors

Michiel van Vreeswijk, MSc, is a clinical psychologist, psychothera-pist, cognitive-behavioral therapist, certified supervisor in schema ther-apy and co-director at G-kracht mental health care institute, The Netherlands. He is affiliated as a trainer in schema therapy and cogni-tive-behavior therapy at several post-doctoral institutes for psychologists and psychiatrists in The Netherlands. He is also affiliated with the RINO Group as main lecturer of psycho-diagnostic assessment. He regularly gives schema therapy workshops in the UK, Germany, other countries, and at conferences of the International Society of Schema Therapy (ISST). He researches schema group therapy and is the (co-)author of many journal articles and books in English, German and Dutch.

    Jenny Broersen, MSc, is a mental health care psychologist and psychotherapist. She is a supervisor in cognitive-behavior therapy and schema therapy (Dutch register Schema Therapy and International Society of Schema Therapy). During the last 15 years she has worked in outpatient and day treatment settings. Broersen is the site director of G-kracht psychomedisch centrum BV in Amsterdam, together with her colleague Marjon Nadort. She also works in the mental health care insti-tute GGZ Delfland in Delft (The Netherlands). She is co-author/editor of several schema books, chapters, and articles and gives post-doctoral courses in schema therapy and cognitive-behavior therapy.

Ger Schurink, MSc, is a psychotherapist, health psychologist, and cognitive-behavioral therapist. He is a certified supervisor in cognitive-behavior therapy, has a private practice in The Netherlands, and is a trainer in Mindfulness Based Cognitive Therapy. He is the (co-)author of several books and articles.

Foreword

The field of psychological science is undergoing something of a revolution in the way it sees the origin and maintenance of emotional problems. From this vision a new way of helping those people who come to therapy is emerging. This book contributes to this development.

In the 1970s and 1980s the main concern of research in clinical psychology was to investigate biases in information processing. The field was dominated by experiments demonstrating, again and again, the extent to which people suffering from depression or from anxiety disorders of various kinds, showed biases in the way they attended to their internal or external environment; biases in the way they remembered the past or anticipated the future; biases in their judgments and interpretations. Part of this approach was research on schemas. Schemas are information-processing structures that normally assist in the streamlining of encoding and retrieval of complex sets of information. Such structures are enormously valuable in making cognitive processing efficient, but they can also make habitual the biases that are seen elsewhere in the information-processing system, establishing them into a biased sense of "self," "me," and "how I am." When such patterns of processing become automatic in this way, these habitual reactions in thinking, feeling, and interacting with the world coalesce to form higher-order patterns: this we label "personality."

This phase of the development of cognition and emotion research was hugely influential and highly productive in terms of its effects on cognitive and behavioral approaches. Yet gradually, as more research was done, we saw that there were other elements in the picture. In particular, we began to see that the ways people *react* to their own biased processing could determine whether the reaction would be maintained and exacerbate, or extinguish and fade. It was found that emotional problems were often maintained not only by the bias in attention, memory, judgments, or schemas, but by the processes that "come on line" to try and deal with such biases. Chief among these are two processes: the tendency to elaborate, become enmeshed in, or ruminate about things on the one hand; and the tendency to avoid, suppress, and push things away on the other. Dealing with these tendencies had always been implicit within cognitive and behavioral approaches, but the increasing awareness of the power of these ruminative and avoidance processes gave a new impetus to attempts to find explicit ways of dealing with them.

Mindfulness training is one such approach. It invites us to learn how to attend, first to moment-by-moment experience (internal or external), and then to see clearly how the mind can be caught up in elaboration or avoidance. Gradually, through such training, we learn to broaden awareness so we can see how a whole *mode of mind* is activated when things don't go the way we want them to go, and how this "doing" mode, so useful in many circumstances, does not serve us when we are trying our best to deal with difficult and destructive emotions. In mindfulness training, by seeing the patterns of the mind more clearly, we are better able to make choices about what action, if any, to take. What emerges is a sense of having more space, having a greater capacity for wisdom and a deeper sense of compassion for the self and for others. Together with other new approaches that focus on dealing skilfully with rumination and avoidance, and approaches that cultivate acceptance, commitment, and compassion, mindfulness approaches are changing the way we think about emotion, and about what it is that any of us needs when the "storms in the mind" are raging and seem to be beyond our control. The evidence from clinical trials shows that the mindfulness approach can have large effects on alleviating emotional problems, and this book is an important next step toward clarifying what is most helpful for whom under what circumstances.

Mark Williams
Author of *The Mindful Way Through
Depression: Freeing Yourself From
Chronic Unhappiness*

Acknowledgments

This book incorporates many insights developed by other researchers and practitioners. We would especially like to thank Segal, Williams, and Teasdale, for their permission to use several exercises from their book, *Mindfulness-Based Cognitive Therapy for Depression* (2002). The exercises were slightly adjusted to suit the purposes of this book. We also extend thanks to Bennett-Goldman for letting us edit material from her book (*Emotional Alchemy*, 2001). We thank Susan Simpson for editing the English text.

Last but not least, we want to thank our patients for providing us with the opportunity to mindfully observe how, and what, they themselves observed. Many of their annotations, implicit and explicit, have been assimilated into this work.

Michiel van Vreeswijk
Jenny Broersen
Ger Schurink

Part I
Theoretical Background

1

Introduction

Patients with personality problems are often affected by excessive emotion or, conversely, a lack of affect. Schema Therapy is about linking emotions with the triggering of schemas and modes. Through the use of cognitive-behavioral therapy techniques, experiential therapy, and interpersonal practices like limited reparenting, patients learn how to assign new meaning to their emotions and approach them in new ways. Increasingly, Schema Therapy is beginning to include mindfulness techniques in its therapeutic toolbox (e.g. see Van Genderen & Arntz, 2009; Van Vreeswijk, Broersen, & Nadort, 2012; Young, Klosko, & Weishaar, 2003). These techniques are deemed experiential in form. To date, training protocols for mindfulness in Schema Therapy have not yet been established, but the techniques to be involved in such training have been implemented in treatment with a variety of psychiatric disorders, with considerable success.

This protocol contains clear guidelines for providing mindfulness training to patients struggling with schemas and modes. Central to

Mindfulness and Schema Therapy: A Practical Guide, First Edition.
Michiel van Vreeswijk, Jenny Broersen and Ger Schurink.
© 2014 John Wiley & Sons, Ltd. Published 2014 by John Wiley & Sons, Ltd.

this practice is the development of attention skills. Patients are encouraged to practice observing the operation of schemas and modes, and to notice their automatic effects on behavior. Rather than attempting to change how they work, training focuses on cultivating awareness of schemas and modes. Additional areas of attention include the monitoring of emotions, physical sensations, and schema-coping mechanisms.

The protocol lays out a comprehensive program consisting of eight sessions and two follow-up sessions. It is presumed that training will be offered in a group setting, but it can be applied just as easily on an individual basis. At the following website, http://www.mfvanvreeswijk.com, patients can buy mindfulness exercises (audio files), like the ones in this book. We consider these required listening, as experience has shown the training to be more effective when participants practice on their own, outside of the group meetings.

For some patients this protocol will run concurrently with existing (Schema) therapy. Others may not yet have commenced treatment, in which case the development of schema and mode awareness will better prepare them for therapy. Certain individuals will no longer require treatment subsequent to participation in mindfulness training. This may be the case with patients who report relatively mild levels of distress or show limited motivation for treatment.

This book employs the term *participant* as well as *patient*. A conscious decision was made to use the term participant in chapters describing the mindfulness training protocol, and the term patient in others. This designation is based on the functional distinction between patients, who sign up for training, and participants, who engage in training. For the same reasons, the term *therapist* is replaced with *trainer* in chapters dealing with the protocol.

We will not delve into any in-depth discussions of the personality disorders and Schema Therapy literature, as these topics have already enjoyed thorough coverage in other books (e.g., van Vreeswijk, Broersen, & Nadort, 2012). Nor shall we consider the subject of group dynamics. Suffice it to say that experience in group-based therapy and training in personality disorders is vital for those planning to apply this material in group settings. We also recommend training in mindfulness-based cognitive therapy and the book *Mindfulness-Based Cognitive Therapy for Depression*, by Segal, Williams, and Teasdale (2002).

The creation of this protocol was motivated by positive experience with the application of mindfulness techniques in Schema Therapy, even in cases of profound personality disorder. A pre-post study and a randomized controlled trial are currently in progress, and the results will be described in forthcoming articles.

Prior to attending "Training Mindfulness and Schema Therapy," Chantal frequently showed up at the polyclinic or crisis center following a sudden relationship breakup or impulsive self-injury.

During the initial training sessions, Chantal comments on how bored she is with the program. It's not yielding results fast enough for her. The trainers suggest that Chantal practice renewing her focus, moment by moment, on whatever feelings, thoughts, or impulses to act may occur, and to resist her tendency to react. Over the course of the training, the number of crises she reports subsides; during the follow-up period, there are barely any. Although she did not practice all of the material consistently, Chantal now considers the training to have been of great value. She has become more aware of the operation of her schemas and modes and how these put her on automatic pilot. By learning how to recognize and identify schema/mode patterns, she is developing a greater capacity for mindful decision making, reducing the amount of automatic, impulsive behavior.

2

Schema Therapy

Schema Therapy is an integrative system of psychotherapy for people with personality problems and/or enduring Axis I disorders. Developed by Dr. Jeffrey Young (Young, Klosko, & Weishaar, 2003), it incorporates theories and techniques derived from cognitive-behavioral therapy, interpersonal psychotherapy, Gestalt therapy, psychodynamic therapy, and attachment theory (for a detailed description of relevant theory, practice, and research, see Van Genderen & Arntz, 2009; Van Vreeswijk, Broersen, & Nadort, 2012; Young et al., 2003).

Schema and Mode Definitions

Schema Therapy utilizes the concepts of schemas and modes. Schemas are considered to represent the way people perceive themselves, others, and the world around them. They are constructed out of sensory perceptions, emotions, and actions etched into memory during previous experiences, especially in childhood (Arntz, Van Genderen, & Wijts, 2006; Rijkeboer, Van Genderen, & Arntz, 2007; Young et al., 2003).

Mindfulness and Schema Therapy: A Practical Guide, First Edition.
Michiel van Vreeswijk, Jenny Broersen and Ger Schurink.
© 2014 John Wiley & Sons, Ltd. Published 2014 by John Wiley & Sons, Ltd.

While schemas are seen as *trait* features of personality, modes refer to *state* features. Modes are a combination of the schemas and behaviors—adaptive or maladaptive—that are present at any particular moment (Lobbestael, Van Vreeswijk, & Arntz, 2007; Young et al., 2003). Modes can also be seen as the moods in which individuals may dwell for short or longer periods of time, and can alternate or change at the drop of a hat.

Nineteen schemas and twenty modes have been established so far (for an overview, see Table 2.1; for a description of schemas and

Table 2.1 Schemas and modes

Nineteen schemas	*Twenty modes*
Emotional Deprivation	Vulnerable Child
Abandonment/Instability	Angry Child
Mistrust and/or Abuse	Enraged Child
Social Isolation/Alienation	Impulsive Child
Defectiveness/Shame	Undisciplined Child
Social Undesirability	Happy Child
Failure	Compliant Surrender
Dependence/Incompetence	Detached Protector
Vulnerability to Harm and Illness	Detached Self-soother
Enmeshment/Undeveloped Self	Self-Aggrandizer
Subjugation	Bully and Attack
Self-Sacrifice	Punitive Parent
Approval Seeking★	Demanding Parent
Emotional Inhibition	Healthy Adult
Unrelenting Standards/Hypocritical	Angry Protector★★
Negativity and Pessimism★	Obsessive Over-Controller★★
Punitiveness★	Paranoid★★
Entitlement/Grandiosity	Conning and Manipulative★★
Insufficient Self-Control/Self-Discipline	Predator★★
	Attention-seeker★★

★These schemas are not yet identifiable using the Schema Questionnaire (YSQ).
★★These modes have not (yet) been added to the Schema Mode Inventory (SMI-1).
Source: van Vreeswijk, Broersen, and Nadort, 2012. Reproduced with permission of Wiley.

modes, see the patient folder in Appendix II-B). Schemas can be evaluated using the Schema Questionnaire (YSQ-2; Schmidt, Joiner, Young, & Telch, 1995), and modes can be identified using the Schema-Mode Inventory (SMI-1; Young et al., 2007).

Schemas and modes are maintained through various schema coping behaviors, from which three distinct coping styles can be discerned: schema avoidance, schema compensation, and schema surrender. These are defined as follows.

Schema avoidance

The individual attempts to stay out of situations that might trigger the schema, or seeks distractions, in order to avoid thinking about the schema and experiencing related feelings. For instance, someone with the Abandonment/Instability schema will be slow to form attachments with others, because interpersonal bonds entail the possibility of being deserted at a later stage. Such an individual will also try to avoid situations that remind him of past abandonment, so that the feelings connected to those memories remain at bay.

Example—Schema avoidance

Bram has suffered many losses in his life. Shortly after his parents' divorce at age five, Bram's mother died of breast cancer. His father soon developed a new relationship, often leaving Bram alone with the babysitter. Bram initiated treatment after his girlfriend unexpectedly left him. After three months of treatment, his female therapist announces an upcoming six-week vacation. Bram does not show up at the following appointment. He misses the next few sessions, without notifying his therapist. Her phone calls go unanswered, until one day, just before her vacation, she receives an email. Bram writes that he may contact her afterwards, but that, for now, the treatment is causing him too much stress.

Schema compensation

The individual demonstrates the opposite behavior in order to resist the schema. Instead of striving for perfection, someone with the Unrelenting Standards/Hypocritical schema might get sloppy and impulsive, perhaps claiming to enjoy chaos.

Example—Schema compensation

Erica is unfailingly conscientious. Others even find her too conscientious. When Erica finds herself repeatedly hitting a wall at work, reacting to her colleagues' seeming incompetence with increased annoyance, she signs up for therapy. While preparing a case conceptualization, it becomes apparent that Erica holds herself and others to exceedingly high standards. This is one of the reasons for her problems at work. The therapist suspects that additional schemas may be involved, which he suggests they investigate. Because Erica is eager to get results, she announces her recovery to the company physician and returns to work. She proceeds to rush through her tasks, and frequently leaves her files at home or on the train, asserting that she isn't worried about her carelessness. In the next therapy session, Erica seems gloomy, reproachful, and desperate. Her boss has reprimanded her for her sloppiness and she has called in sick again. She hopes the therapist will hurry up and give her some advice, because she is fed up with being unwell.

Schema surrender

The individual behaves in accordance with his schema. He thinks, acts, and feels consistently with the schema. For instance, when the Self-Sacrifice schema is triggered, a person engaging schema surrender as a coping strategy will feel compelled to put the needs and desires of others before his own. He thinks his opinion is unimportant and feels better when accommodating others.

Example—Schema surrender

Alex related the following story to his therapist: Yesterday my girlfriend asked me to pick up some groceries and prepare dinner. So, I left work early and even rescheduled a meeting with my supervisor. When my girlfriend asked me about my day, I told her everything went fine. I told her I hadn't heard anything about the promotion I was lined up for, because I moved the meeting with my boss in order to go grocery shopping. Suddenly my girlfriend became very angry. She found it incredibly stupid that I cancelled the appointment with my supervisor. She said that I'm always busy with other people's business and never with my own. I just looked at her in surprise. Wasn't she the one who asked me to go shopping? So why wouldn't I do that?

A person can employ multiple coping styles. Schema Therapy involves working on improving the way in which schema and mode triggering is handled, and becoming less automatic in the way specific schema coping styles are engaged.

Schema Techniques

Schema Therapy[1] is an integrative approach to treatment that encompasses a variety of techniques from several therapy modalities.

Central to Schema Therapy is the strategy of *limited reparenting*. The therapeutic alliance can have a corrective effect on schemas and modes resulting from early attachment relationships. The therapist is expected to remain active and transparent throughout. Key factors include judicious self-disclosure, discussion of the therapeutic alliance, and uncovering the schemas and modes that are active within this relationship.

Other important techniques in Schema Therapy involve formulating a schema and/or mode-focused case conceptualization, as well as keeping schema and mode journals that stimulate growing awareness of their activation and operation.

The adequacy of schemas and modes can also be examined through the application of cognitive interventions. Examples of cognitive techniques include advantage/disadvantage analysis, piecharts, multi-dimensional evaluation, data collection, and the use of a court-case style approach, in which schemas are accused and must be defended.

Other types of intervention may implement behavioral techniques. For instance, role-playing exercises can be used to help bring awareness to the here-and-now. The patient is asked to act out a situation in which a schema or mode typically becomes active. In the first round of the role-playing exercise, conditions are simulated in such a way as to trigger the schema and/or mode in question. Plenty of space is provided for the patient's emotional experience, with particular attention to any schema behavior that may arise. The patient subsequently repeats the role-playing exercise, but this time attempts to react from the perspective of the Healthy Adult.

Experiential interventions are geared toward the experience and expression of emotions associated with (earlier) situations that have contributed to the development of schemas and modes. Examples of experiential techniques in Schema Therapy include historical role-play exercises, chair work techniques, imagery exercises, expressive therapy (e.g., psychomotor therapy, visual and drama techniques), and schema Mindfulness-Based Cognitive Therapy (sMBCT). In historical role-play, the patient's exposure to a childhood situation is considered, alongside the experience of another individual, often a parent figure (through role reversal). Consequently, the patient learns more adequate ways to respond to the situation. The introduction of the Healthy Adult, who supports the patient and helps him express his needs and desires, is instrumental in the patient's acquisition of more appropriate responses to a specific situation.

In the multiple-chair technique, the patient designates a different chair to each of his modes. This setup facilitates intrapsychic contact. The moment a patient enters a particular mode, the therapist directs the mode to a seat and addresses it from the perspective of the Healthy

11

Adult. This spatial approach creates room for the patient's vulnerable aspects and allows him to confront his basic needs within a controlled environment.

The imagination can thus be used to create a safe space for the patient. It is also employed in the process of *rescripting*. In this case, the patient is asked to recall a memory related to a certain schema. Once the memory has taken shape in his mind, the image of a Healthy Adult is introduced to the scene, such as a kind and caring grand-mother. This imaginary adult then comes to the aid of the Vulnerable Child part of the patient, or provides whatever is needed for the Vulnerable Child to negotiate the situation that is being recalled in imagery.

Art therapy practices (see for example Haeyen, 2007) can similarly be applied to help transform schemas and modes using nonverbal techniques. Along with mindfulness techniques, art therapy approaches to Schema Therapy represent more recent developments in this field.

Research Findings in Schema Therapy

The effectiveness of Schema Therapy in treating borderline person-ality disorder patients has been demonstrated with a randomized controlled trial (Giesen-Bloo et al., 2006), in which Schema Therapy was compared with a form of psychodynamic therapy (Transference-Focused Therapy, TFP). Although both treatment conditions appeared to be effective in treating borderline personality disorder, Schema Therapy resulted in a greater number of full recoveries, a lower dropout rate, and greater cost efficiency (Giesen-Bloo et al., 2006; Van Asselt et al., 2008). A study by Nadort et al. (submitted) investigated the impact on (cost) effectiveness of Schema Therapy with borderline patients in outpatient clinics. Bamelis, Evers, Spinhoven, and Arntz (2014) examined the effects of Schema Therapy with other personality disorders. The use of Schema Therapy in group settings has been under study in several disorders (Farrel, Shaw, & Webber, 2009; Renner et al., 2013; Simpson,

Morrow, Van Vreeswijk, & Reid, 2010; Van Vreeswijk, Spinhoven, Eurlings-Bontekoe, & Broersen, 2012). For a recent overview of the research literature on Schema Therapy see also Van Vreeswijk, Broersen, and Nadort (2012).

Developments in Schema Therapy

The continued development of Schema Therapy was stimulated by the publication of a randomized, multi-center research study on the effectiveness of Schema Therapy in patients with borderline personality disorder (Giesen-Bloo et al., 2006). Schema Therapy has been adapted for relationship therapy (see Atkinson, as cited in Van Vreeswijk et al., 2012), for adolescents (Geerdink, Jongman, & Scholing, 2012; Renner et al., 2013), and for patients in forensic settings (Bernstein, Arntz, & De Vos, 2007). It is increasingly being used by art therapists as well (Haeyen, 2006, 2007).

Note

1. For an exhaustive description of Schema Therapy techniques, see Van Genderen & Arntz, 2009; Van Vreeswijk, Broersen, & Nadort, 2012; Young, Klosko, & Weishaar, 2003.

3

Mindfulness

Mindfulness is a mental state that involves observing and allowing one's thoughts and feelings as they arise in the present. It can be learned through directed attention exercises, and can be integrated with existing therapy methods and training programs for use with many psychological problems.

Central to this practical implementation of mindfulness is developing the ability to recognize old, engrained, and automatic emotional response patterns as they occur. This process requires focused attention on the body's response to emotional patterns. The repeated bringing to awareness and allowance of these patterns gradually leads to acceptance, and creates room for behavioral adjustment. With practice, patients can learn to apply this skill to their own psychological symptoms.

This can be illustrated with an ordinary example. Imagine someone criticizes you. Instantly, you experience an unpleasant state of tension. Thoughts race through your mind as the area around your chest tightens and your heart rate jumps. You feel hot and start to blush, holding back whatever it is you really want to say. Hours later,

Mindfulness and Schema Therapy: A Practical Guide, First Edition.
Michiel van Vreeswijk, Jenny Broersen and Ger Schurink.
© 2014 John Wiley & Sons, Ltd. Published 2014 by John Wiley & Sons, Ltd.

the incident still lingers. You brood over the order of events, what you should have said but didn't dare to, and how you will act differently next time.

Mindfulness helps you to become aware of these kinds of automatic patterns. You learn to recognize the recurring stories in your head, such as "I'm worthless," "I'm incompetent," or "I'm powerless." You notice that the sensations arising in your body are sensations that you *don't* want, and you discover that much of your thought and behavior is aimed at getting rid of those unpleasant and painful feelings.

We are perpetually in *doing-mode*; always busy thinking and acting toward some objective. Meditation teaches us to enter *being-mode*, and to remain there. We permit every experience, including those we do not want, repeatedly reacting out of habit or impulse. Through this process our old and engrained response patterns lose their power over us, and we cultivate the freedom to respond differently.

Origins of Mindfulness-Based Treatment Methods

The mindfulness training presented and discussed in this book is derived from Mindfulness-Based Cognitive Therapy (MBCT). Beginning in 1995, MBCT was developed as a training program for groups of patients with recurrent depression. In recent years it has increasingly found application in individual settings and the focus of treatment has expanded to include other types of disorder (Teasdale, Segal, & Williams, 1995).

In the West, interest in meditation as a therapeutic approach began to emerge in the 1960s (Germer, 2005). Jon Kabat-Zinn was a pioneer who applied this form of meditation in a medical setting with patients experiencing pain and psychosomatic symptoms. Kabat-Zinn's methodology, named Mindfulness-Based Stress Reduction (MBSR, Kabat-Zinn, 1990), involves an intensive mindfulness training program consisting of eight weeks of weekly three-hour sessions, in which patients learn assorted meditation techniques as well as yoga exercises.

Teasdale and colleagues (1995) have also performed pioneering work in this area. The lack of a successful system for treating recurrent depression motivated them to develop Mindfulness-Based Cognitive Therapy (MBCT). They integrated MBSR and cognitive-behavioral therapy techniques in order to help prevent relapse in patients with a history of three or more episodes of depression. Their program yielded positive results. In a post-treatment follow-up period of 60 weeks, the percentage of relapses of depression was reduced to approximately half, compared to the control group, which was given treatment-as-usual (Ma & Teasdale, 2004; Teasdale et al., 2000).

These early research findings have led to a surge of enthusiasm and optimism about potential applications of mindfulness techniques. Hundreds of popular books on mindfulness have been published, and the expanding body of research literature on mindfulness-based treatment covers a range of topics, including qualitative research, controlled clinical trials, and neuroscientific studies. Black (2013) appraises the number of scientific publications appearing each year, showing an increase from 28 articles in 2002 to as many as 397 by 2011. Many of these studies demonstrate the positive effects of mindfulness-based interventions.

The success of mindfulness in clinical practice coincides with the advent of a new paradigm in treatment methodology. This development is expertly illustrated by Hayes (2005), who distinguishes between three generations of behavioral therapy. The first generation saw the dawning of behavioral therapy. This form of treatment is typified by its emphasis on the psychological principles of learning, such as classical and operant conditioning. The arrival of the cognitive revolution in psychology paved the way for cognitive-behavioral therapy, the second generation. Its principal assumption is that psychological problems arise or are perpetuated by the disturbance of specific cognitive functions and schemas. Treatment is directed toward changing dysfunctional thoughts, with the goal of eradicating or gaining control of maladaptive behavior. The third generation of treatment approaches is not as much about changing dysfunctional thoughts, feelings, and behavior, as it is about changing one's *attitude* toward them. This "third wave" is currently made up of four fully functioning systems of treatment that have been evaluated for effectiveness, and in which mindfulness plays an important role: Mindfulness-Based Stress Reduction (MBSR), Mindfulness-Based Cognitive Therapy (MBCT), Dialectical Behavioral Therapy (DBT), and Acceptance and Commitment Therapy (ACT).

Besides the above, there are several other mindfulness-based interventions (MBIs) and treatment protocols in which mindfulness is integrated with cognitive-behavioral therapy. Segal, Williams, and Teasdale (2002) predicted that mindfulness-based treatment programs would lead to sweeping changes in the therapy profession. Their prediction was more accurate than they had imagined: In the second, revised edition of the authoritative book, *Mindfulness-Based Cognitive Therapy for Depression* (2013), the authors indicate an unexpected explosion of interest in the use of mindfulness in treating a great number of physical and psychological conditions.

Definitions

Simply stated, in the context of MBCT, mindfulness is defined as (a) being observant of all that is experienced (sensory perception, thoughts, and feelings), and (b) permitting all experience including thoughts (analyzing, planning, fantasizing, judging, reasoning), behaviors, and behavioral urges (avoidance behavior, distraction seeking) without reacting automatically to it.

However, the term mindfulness is often used in different ways, which may lead to some confusion. Several definitions exist, depending on the context of its use: as a meditation technique (formal mindfulness meditation), as a state of mind (being mindful), as a trait, as a skill (mindful reaction), and as a treatment method (therapeutic application).

In light of the ambiguity of the construct, experts in the field of mindfulness-based therapy have organized consensus conferences aimed at establishing an operational definition of the term. Bishop et al. (2004) describe mindfulness as a continuum of mental processes that serves to understand how functional and dysfunctional thoughts, feelings, and behaviors arise, with the goal of strengthening the former and attenuating the latter. They propose an operational definition of mindfulness based on two components. The first component concerns the *self-regulation of attention*, which entails directing attention at sensory experiences and mental events arising in the present moment. The second component describes an *orientation to experience* that is open and inviting; every thought, feeling, and physical sensation is accepted, without expressing intentional judgment and without wishing to change it.

Self-regulation of attention

Directing attention is the first step. The aim is to maintain conscious awareness, from moment to moment, of that which presents itself in the form of thought and sensation. This may involve a broad and all-encompassing sort of attention, or a focus on specific phenomena, such as the body's emotional response. Steady and constant concentration is required. A common device used to aid concentration is the centering of awareness in the breath. The experience of breathing thus becomes a focal point for attention.

An important element in this practice is the capacity to recognize when distractions occur, and then directly returning to the intended subject of awareness. The core skill to be developed in mindfulness is that of turning off the "automatic pilot," circumventing the habitual tendency toward unconscious reaction (Segal, Williams, & Teasdale, 2002). Mindfulness effectively fosters meta-awareness: the human mind's capacity to observe itself and its behavior, and to contemplate personal actions and situations as though from a distance. Meta-awareness allows us to switch from automatic pilot to manual control.

Orientation to experience

The second component of mindfulness is the cultivation of an open and accepting attitude toward thoughts, feelings, and physical responses. Acceptance happens when unpleasantness is allowed to

18

exist, without limitation, without evaluation, and without attempts to hold on or to resist. Such an attitude stands in direct opposition to our usual orientation: judgment, leading to action. Segal, Williams, and Teasdale (2013) refer to this as the *doing mode*, which is automatically activated when the brain detects a discrepancy between our current state and a desired state. This becomes most apparent when unpleasant thoughts and/or feelings arise. Explanations for the discomfort are sought, along with solutions to the problem perceived, in an effort to avoid further distress. If more urgent tasks demand attention, the problem is dealt with later on, but only after a solution has been found will the unpleasantness cease. Keywords related to the doing-mode include analyzing, judging, evaluating, solving, achieving, testing, planning, pursuing goals, adjusting, and obsessing. The doing-mode is suitable for practical, technical, and intellectual tasks, but is also so entrenched that it is activated to handle emotional problems as well.

When emotions are involved, the *being-mode*, which in many ways represents the opposite of the doing-mode, is more appropriate. The being mode is characterized by non-judging, permitting, non-striving, acceptance, understanding through direct experience, and a broad focusing of awareness (Segal, Williams, & Teasdale, 2013).

Mindfulness Exercises and Applications

In mindfulness-based therapy, treatment revolves around mindfulness training and its implementation in situations that trigger inadequate responses or psychological problems. MBSR, and MBCT in particular, routinely incorporate formal meditation exercises of up to 45 minutes per day. In contrast, ACT and DGT methods make use of psychoeducation and a host of exercises for promoting mindfulness, but involve little meditative practice.

This chapter covers several meditation exercises with practical applications, all of which have in common the same basic instructions and objectives. We will first discuss the most widely used mindfulness technique, breathing meditation, followed by a number of other meditation exercises and their application.

Breathing meditation

Sitting upright in a relaxed and alert position, attention is focused on the physical sensation of breathing. Attention tends to get sidetracked quite easily. When this occurs, instructions are simply to notice the distraction in a gentle, non-judging manner, and to bring awareness back to the principal object of attention. In this case, the objective is not exclusively to focus on the breath. In fact, the actual awareness of breathing becomes the primary medium for the development of an open and perceptive stance, from which everything is experienced without following habitual reactions. In other words, one's thoughts, feelings, and impulses are merely observed. They are not ignored, analyzed, or suppressed, but are permitted—without subsequent action and without losing awareness of the breath. Unequivocally, this is an exercise in turning off the automatic pilot and stepping out of doing mode. Patients are encouraged to practice this skill in daily life as often as possible, especially when dysfunctional emotional patterns threaten to surface. In this way, mindfulness creates a time-out between an experience and the immediate reaction it provokes. It facilitates a switch, as it were, from automatic transmission to manual, granting the freedom and space to react differently to whatever happens. More detailed and precise descriptions of mindfulness meditation can be found in Gunaratana (2011), Smalley and Winston (2010), and Segal, Williams, and Teasdale (2013).

Body-focused meditation

This involves focusing awareness on one's perception of the body, which may present purely physical sensations, such as the body's contact with the seat, or somatic emotional responses, such as tension around the chest.

There are two variants of this exercise. In the body scan meditation, awareness is progressively moved through parts of the body.

The other variant is based on a broad, open form of attention to the body as a whole. If one particular physical sensation is in the foreground, it remains the point of focus until another sensation attracts attention.

The instruction is to continually observe and allow perceptions that arise, without doing anything about them.

Meditation focused on various objects

Besides the breath and other bodily phenomena, attention can be focused on sounds, thoughts representing words or phrases (internal speech), or on thoughts in the form of images (memories and fantasies). Another kind of meditation exercise is choiceless awareness (or mindfulness without an object), in which attention is broad and all-encompassing. There is no focal point, and anything goes. Whatever appears in awareness also disappears, and does so without intervention.

Meditation in movement

Walking meditation is a widely practiced technique, and can be a valuable alternative to seated meditation. While walking, attention is initially turned toward the soles of the feet and gradually expanded to the rest of the body. Walking meditation, and other types of meditation involving movement, can be performed slowly or at the accustomed pace. These kinds of exercises are an effective way of involving mindfulness techniques in day-to-day life.

Mindfulness in daily activities

In addition to the aforementioned exercises, which are meant to be performed daily and at specifically allotted times, there are also ways to practice mindfulness during regular day-to-day activities and tasks.

Special attention can be given to routine actions, like tooth brushing, showering, dish washing, walking up and down stairs, and eating. Spontaneous moments in the day may also provide opportunities for practice, for instance, while waiting in a queue, walking short distances, or answering the phone. Another mindfulness exercise calls for occasional breaks over the course of the day. One momentarily concentrates on the sensation of breathing, followed by a focus on whatever happens to be active in one's experience at the time. The objective is not to react automatically and impulsively, but rather to notice stimuli before they are responded to.

Breathing space

Three Minute Breathing Space is a specialized mindfulness application developed by Segal et al. (2002, 2013). This exercise is meant to be employed when habitual patterns are triggered in daily life. The breathing space provides patients with an opportunity to step out of automatic pilot mode when situations require conscious consideration. The exercise is made up of three steps, each taking approximately one minute to complete. The first step is the bringing into awareness of any bodily sensations, thoughts, or feelings coming into being. In the second step, attention is focused as much as possible on the experience of breathing. In the third step, attention is expanded to the full physical presence, with the breath remaining in background awareness. A phrase that may be recited is "It's okay ... whatever it is, it's already here: let me feel it" (Williams, Teasdale, Segal, & Kabat-Zinn, 2007).

Mindfulness meditation regarding a specific issue

An emotionally laden issue can also become the object of meditation (Segal, Williams, and Teasdale, 2013). In this exercise, the instruction is to divide attention between the sensation of breathing and locations in the body where emotional responses are most pronounced. If emotions become overwhelming, then awareness can be temporarily focused on the breath.

22

Mindful exposure

If any presently taxing experiences or traumatic memories come up, then the therapist can supervise an exercise in mindful exposure. An image is selected that best reflects the patient's unpleasant experience. The therapist then asks the patient to report his or her physical sensations at 10- to 20-second intervals. The patient is instructed to accept everything that emerges, and to do nothing in response. Although behavioral therapy and mindful exposure have some procedures in common, their basic instructions differ on important points. The typical explanation for exposure in behavioral therapy is: "If you persist in the confrontation with your problematic (usually frightening) situation, you will notice that your emotional response will subside, and that your (usually anxiety-provoking) expectation will not materialize." In other words, the unpleasant feeling is expected to fade through habituation and irrational thoughts to disappear accordingly. This is not the standpoint of mindful exposure. Just as with other mindfulness exercises, the instructions are to allow feelings to arise and to focus on their physical responses—to expect nothing, and to do nothing. In the long run, paradoxically, transformation is achieved by letting go. The goal, then, is not to regulate the frequency and intensity of emotions, but to foster an open and accepting attitude toward them.

The selection and planning of meditation exercises depend on the nature of the problem, the treatment plan, the patient's wishes, and the options available. Bringing mindfulness-based techniques into therapy can take the form of a complete training program that incorporates all of the practices described above, or may be limited to the application of a small number of exercises in tandem with some existing treatment plan (Rapgay et al., 2013).

Mindfulness exercise duration

The recommended duration of mindfulness exercises in the context of training and therapy ranges from 30 to 45 minutes, both in session and on a daily basis between meetings. Also recommended is continuation of daily mindfulness practice after the training has ended. Carmody and Baer (2009) performed a meta-analysis of 30 studies which showed that practitioners advocate an average of 45 minutes of practice per day, 6 days a week. Training participants are also asked to practice mindfulness skills during daily activities, which is known as informal practice. Additionally, many MBSR training programs include a day of silence, and both practitioners and instructors are advised to regularly attend multi-day meditation retreats as a way to increase their expertise. These extended retreats are commonly practiced for spiritual purposes, but have been adopted in the field of mindfulness-based psychotherapy. There seems to be a common assumption that frequent and long-lasting meditation is necessary, yet scientific studies demonstrate that more is not always better.

Research findings suggest that the relationship between the duration and effect of mindfulness exercise (both formal and informal) is unclear or does not exist. Davidson et al. (2003) studied the neurological and biological changes that occur following mindfulness training and found no significant relationship between exercise length and associated changes. Nor was any such correlation found in Hölzel et al.'s (2011) study on mindfulness in the brain.

A recent study by Klatt, Buckworth, and Malarkey (2008) assessed a shortened MBSR training program for professionals. Participants meditated at work for 20 minutes at a time, 5 days a week, for a sum total of 6 hours, whereas the standard MBSR training program entails more than 20 hours of practice over 10 weeks. The shorter training was found to have significant effects on measures like stress and quality of sleep, and these effects were comparable to those of the standard training.

A meta-analysis by Vettese, Toneatto, Stea, Nguyen, and Wang (2009) incorporated 24 studies that provided data on exercise duration and outcomes. The average time spent on mindfulness practice was 31.8 minutes per day, with a range from 5 to 58 minutes. According to Vettese, nearly half of the studies showed no support for the hypothesis that longer exercises yield better results. Studies that did support the link between duration and outcome employed many self-selected participants and participants active in healthcare. This suggests that positive expectations and previous exposure to mindfulness may have been (partly) responsible for these results.

Perich, Manacavasgar, Mitchell, and Ball (2013) performed a study on the use of MBCT with bipolar disorder, in which pre- and post-training measurements indicated no relationship between duration of mindfulness practice and psychiatric symptoms. Furthermore, follow-up tests administered 12 months after training showed no significant improvement of symptoms in participants who continued practicing mindfulness compared to those who did not.

In their conclusions of a meta-analysis involving 39 studies and a total of 1,140 participants, Hofmann, Sawyer, Witt, and Oh (2010) wrote that mindfulness-based treatments had a robust positive effect on anxiety and mood disorders regardless of training duration. Most training programs consisted of eight meetings with a range of six to twelve sessions. Many programs also included a retreat lasting one day or half a day. Bowen and Kurz (2012) found that the amount of practice between sessions in an eight-week program was positively related to the degree of mindfulness measured upon conclusion of the training, but no such effect was found at two- and four-month follow-ups.

A recently published meta-analysis (Khoury et al., 2013) found no consistent relationship between the number of training sessions and assigned exercises and MBI outcomes. There was, however, a correlation between training outcomes and the therapist's level experience with mindfulness. The authors list group cohesion and quality of practice as additional factors.

In practice, therapists frequently receive feedback from patients regarding their difficulty fitting extended exercises into their day-to-day schedules. Over the course of therapy and in follow-up sessions it typically becomes known that many patients do not carry out their longer exercises in full, whereas shorter exercises such as the Three Minute Breathing Space technique are more compatible with busy schedules. Shorter meditations (8 to 15 minutes) are thus more likely to meet practical considerations such as the need for regular practice and treatment compliance.

Scientific studies and practical experience point to a need for further research on the relationship between exercise duration and effectiveness, and on the necessity of continued practice subsequent to therapy or training. Additionally, there are few data on the effectiveness and duration of mindfulness practice in terms of specific disorders and populations. At present it appears most prudent to select more feasible—and thus shorter—mindfulness techniques in lieu of prolonged exercises that are difficult to combine with everyday life. Advising patients to continue practicing mindfulness once training or therapy has ended is not supported by the literature to date.

Finally, the specific nature of the client's problems and (dis)abilities should be taken into account when selecting mindfulness exercises and exercise lengths. For beginner meditators, greater awareness is often accompanied by increased experience of unpleasant feelings. If this becomes problematic, for instance, when symptoms include anxiety around bodily phenomena (as in hypochondriasis and panic disorder), shorter exercises should be offered. In such cases attention can initially be restricted to external stimuli (sounds) or can focus on movement and/or mindfulness with daily activities. Exercises involving awareness of bodily sensations can be introduced at a later stage. Chadwick, Newman Taylor, and Abba (2005) describes the development of his mindfulness program for psychotic patients: Over the course of four years, the duration of mindfulness exercises had to be reduced from prolonged meditations to a feasible length of just four minutes.

Mindfulness in Schema Therapy

Schema Therapy works in two stages: the assessment stage, in which schemas and modes are identified; and the transformation stage, in which empathic confrontation and reality testing are employed toward the transformation of schemas and modes. Techniques used for modifying schemas and modes are borrowed from cognitive-behavioral therapy (cognitive reorganization, creation of an internalized *healthy voice*, and behavioral exercises designed to disrupt dysfunctional behavior); from experiential therapy (practicing the expression of anger, sadness, or pain); from Gestalt therapy; and from interpersonal psychotherapy techniques.

The mindfulness-based approach introduces a third stage: through nonjudgmental attention to the inner experience of schema and mode activation, room is created for novel ways of responding. This attention-oriented process is illustrated in the example of Anna:

> Anna has just experienced an unpleasant altercation with her 16-year-old daughter. She furiously throws on her coat and leaves for work, much earlier than planned. Riding her bike to the office, she notices all the angry thoughts racing through her mind, and senses an awful tension in her body. She tries to analyze what happened, mulling over ways to handle the situation. Then Anna realizes that her schema has been triggered (Unrelenting standards). Her first reaction is to focus on her breathing, followed by the sensation of riding her bike. Once she has entered a mindful state, she expands her attention to include the rest of her body. Her accelerated heart rate, rapid breathing, and tensed-up muscles come into conscious awareness. Anna gradually recognizes how sad and anxious she is.
>
> Moments later, with memories and fantasies welling up inside, she notices her mind has wandered back to this morning's incident. Determined to stay on track, Anna gets a grip on herself. Every time she finds herself getting lost in thought, she realizes that her schema is active, so she focuses on breathing, biking, and on her body.
>
> Anna continues this process until she arrives at the office. Now the job requires her full attention, so her heated reaction fades

into the background. When her emotions flare up again during a lull in the day's activities, she reconnects with her breath and body until she is able to include her work in this mindful state.

Anna uses this exercise to practice breaking out of her usual pattern of controlling her feelings and pushing them out. When she gets home, she doesn't know what to say to her daughter. This time she can't rely on the mental rehearsals that normally occupy her mind after clashes with other people. Instead of her customary reaction of "telling it like it is," she enters a space from which she can accept her feelings and tell her daughter how much she regrets what took place. When her daughter agrees, they have a good warm hug.

Through this experience, and others like it, Anna comes to realize an important development: She is increasingly able to recognize her schema and tolerate overwhelming emotions, which creates room for her to respond in healthier ways.

Research on Mindfulness with Mental Disorder

Most mindfulness training takes the form of MBSR or MBCT. In its initial development MBSR was geared toward people with physical symptoms (chronic pain/stress) and has therefore found broad application. MBCT was specifically developed for people with recurrent depression. Though primarily used within this population, it is increasingly implemented in the treatment of other mental disorders.

Research on the therapeutic action of mindfulness has gotten off to a strong start, but applications in the domain of several specific disorders have not yet been examined through randomized controlled trials (RCTs). Nonetheless, the literature contains many publications concerning other implementations, noncontrolled studies, and case studies (a recent overview can be found in Baer, 2010). Various studies, most of them RCTs and meta-analyses, are discussed in the following subsections.

Depression

The rise of MBCT followed the success of two randomized trials demonstrating the effectiveness of MBCT as a method for relapse prevention in recurrent depression. Teasdale et al.'s (2000) study involved 145 patients with two or more depressive episodes, with the control group receiving "treatment as usual (TAU)." The mindfulness-based intervention was not found to be more effective than TAU for patients with only two episodes, but showed a significantly greater effect in patients with three or more episodes. Over a period of 60 weeks, 37% of the MBCT group experienced a relapse, compared to 66% relapse in the control group. The second study by Ma and Teasdale (2004) involving 75 patients yielded similar results: a 36% relapse rate in the MBCT group and 78% in the control group. Numerous studies have replicated these results since 2000, all supporting the effectiveness of mindfulness with recurrent depression. A recent RCT involving patients with three or more previous relapses (both with and without current episodes) compared MBCT to a control group (Van Aalderen et al., 2012). Depressive symptoms were significantly reduced by the end of the treatment. Patients reported significantly less worrying and rumination, demonstrated significantly improved mindfulness skills, and reported significantly higher scores for quality of life. MBCT resulted in similar symptom reductions in patients both with and without current depressive episodes.

Piet and Hougaard (2011) performed a meta-analysis of six RCTs with MBCT. Patients with recurrent depression in the MBCT group had a significantly smaller probability of relapsing than controls; the greatest difference was found among patients with three or more depressive episodes.

Eight of the studies included in Klainin-Yobas, Cho, and Creedy's (2012) meta-analysis examined the effects of MBSR on depressive symptoms in people with mental disorders. MBSR appears to be an effective treatment for reducing depressive symptoms in people with mental disorders, demonstrating outcomes similar to those of cognitive-behavioral therapy. Klainin-Yobas et al.'s (2012) study also included 22 studies on the effect of MBCT on depression in people with diverse mental disorders. MBCT was found to have a medium effect size in reducing depressive symptoms.

An RCT by Geschwind, Peeters, Huibers, van Os, and Wichers (2012) looked at residual depression symptoms following at least one depressive episode. Patients were assigned either to an MBCT group (plus standard treatment) or to a control group (waitlist or continued standard treatment). MBCT was found to be significantly better at reducing residual depressive symptoms than the control group. No significant difference was found between persons with one or two episodes and those with three or more.

Anxiety disorders

Vøllestad, Nielsen, and Nielsen's (2012) meta-analysis incorporated four studies that examined the effect of MBSR on anxiety symptoms in people with diverse anxiety disorders (social phobia, panic disorder, generalized anxiety disorder, concurrent depression and anxiety). Each of these studies supported the effectiveness of MBSR in reducing anxiety symptoms; this effect was significant in three of the four studies. Vøllestad et al. (2012) also examined the effects of MBCT on anxiety. Their meta-analysis included nine studies in which anxiety symptoms were reduced as a result of MBCT, with significant effects in four of these studies.

Social phobia  *exercise*

Jazaieri, Goldin, Werner, Ziv, and Gross (2012) led an RCT on MBSR for people with social phobia, comparing the effects of MBSR to an active control group in which participants exercised at a gym at least twice a week for eight weeks. MBSR led to reductions in self-reported anxiety, depression, and stress symptoms upon completion of the training and at a three-month follow-up; increases in well-being were recorded at the same measurement times. Exercise also resulted in reductions in self-reported anxiety, depression, and stress symptoms upon completion of the training and at a three-month follow-up; increases in well-being were recorded at these same measurement times. No significant differences were found between the two interventions. The authors conclude that both MBSR and exercise can contribute to reduction of clinical symptoms in adults with social phobias.

Hypochondriasis/health anxiety

McManus et al. (2012) researched the effects of MBCT (along with standard treatment) on health anxiety, comparing it to a control group that received standard treatment only. MBCT participants showed significantly lower health anxiety than controls, both directly post-intervention and one year after. Significantly fewer participants in the MBCT group than in the control group fulfilled diagnostic criteria for hypochondriasis directly post-intervention as well as one year later (36.1% vs. 76.3%). The authors conclude that MBCT can be a useful supplement to standard treatment for people with health anxiety.

Meta-analyses involving heterogeneous mental health diagnoses

Biegel, Brown, Shapiro, and Schubert's (2009) RCT investigated the effect of MBSR on heterogeneous mental disorders (mood disorders, anxiety disorders, V-code disorders, and other disorders) in adolescents. In this study, MBSR (in addition to standard treatment) was compared to standard treatment alone (individual or group therapy and/or medication). Compared to controls, the MBSR group demonstrated a significantly greater reduction in diagnoses (percentage change) over the course of the five-month study, along with significantly increased Global Assessment of Functioning (GAF) scores. Participants in the MBSR group also indicated significantly fewer self-reported symptoms of anxiety, depression, and somatization, along with increased self-confidence. Effect sizes for these changes in self-reported symptoms were consistently large. The authors conclude that MBSR can be an effective supplement to treatment of adolescents with heterogeneous mental disorders.

A meta-analysis by Hofmann et al. (2010) incorporated 39 studies with a total of 1,140 participants who received mindfulness-based treatment for a variety of complaints, ranging from cancer-related psychological problems, generalized anxiety disorder, depression, and other psychiatric symptoms. The authors report the following results: mindfulness-based therapy had on average a strong, positive effect on anxiety and mood symptoms in all of the studies included in the meta-analysis. Large effects were measured in patients with anxiety and mood disorders as their primary diagnoses, and these effects remained when measured at (on average) 12-week follow-ups.

A recent meta-analysis by Khoury et al. (2013) reviewed 209 studies with a total of 12,145 participants engaging in mindfulness-based therapy (MBT) for various psychological problems. The results indicated that MBT had a medium effect size overall. MBT was not found to be more effective than cognitive-behavioral therapy. However, MBT showed large and clinically relevant effects in treating anxiety and depression, and these effects were maintained at follow-up measurement. Additionally, MBT had fewer dropouts compared to cognitive-behavioral therapy, which suggests greater motivation among MBT participants.

A full description of the effects of mindfulness with all possible disorders lies beyond the scope of this chapter. An up-to-date overview of virtually all relevant studies can be found on the website http://www.mindfulexperience.org. The Mindfulness Research Guide on this website is a comprehensive electronic resource and publication database that provides information to researchers, practitioners, and the general public on the scientific study of mindfulness, including a database of research publications in the area of mindfulness, measurement tools to operationalize mindfulness, interventions incorporating mindfulness techniques, and universities and centers conducting mindfulness research.

In sum, research findings to date support mindfulness-based interventions as an effective supplement to existing treatment methods.

Measuring mindfulness

A number of questionnaires have been developed toward the study of specific aspects of mindfulness and for the assessment of mindfulness-enhancing exercises. At present there are at least seven different questionnaires for measuring mindfulness, of which the most prominent are listed below. The Mindfulness Attention and Awareness Scale (MAAS; Brown & Ryan, 2003) is a self-report questionnaire designed to measure an individual's capacity for maintaining attention and resisting distraction. The Toronto Mindfulness Scale (TMS; Bishop, 2004) is administered directly after meditation and measures attention to internal stimuli and responsiveness. The Kentucky Inventory of Mindfulness Skills (KIMS; Baer, Smith, & Allen, 2004) measures four factors: observing, describing, acting with awareness, and accepting without judgment. The Freiburg Mindfulness Inventory (FMI; Buchheld, Grossman, & Walach, 2011) measures awareness of the present moment, nonjudging acceptance of self and others, openness to negative mental states, and insight.

Although there is consensus among researchers regarding the two most important factors of mindfulness (attention and an accepting attitude), it remains debated how these factors can be measured reliably. For research on the psychometric qualities of various mindfulness-questionnaires, refer to Baer, Smith, Hopkins, Krietemeyer, and Toney (2006).

Baer et al. (2006) investigated the structure of the mindfulness construct on the basis of five recently developed questionnaires. They conclude that there are five facets to mindfulness: describing, acting with awareness, nonjudging, nonreactivity, and observing. Describing is the labeling of experience using words. Acting with awareness means performing actions with active attention. Nonjudging is the absence of positive or negative commentary on thoughts and feelings. Nonreactivity is the permitting of feelings and thoughts without responding to them on automatic pilot. Observing entails remaining conscious of experiences, even when unpleasant or painful. Acceptance is regarded as a result, rather than a facet of mindfulness. Acceptance

33

of anxiety, for instance, develops under the conditions of nonjudging and the absence of impulsive, anxiety-based reactions.

Items in the instruments examined by Baer et al. which best measured the five facets of mindfulness were combined to form the Five Facet Mindfulness Questionnaire (FFMQ; Baer et al., 2006). According to the authors, this questionnaire is internally and conceptually consistent with the elements of mindfulness as described in published literature. The FFMQ's ability to separately measure distinct facets of mindfulness lends itself to research investigating the determinants of positive psychological change in mindfulness-based interventions (Baer, 2010). Empirical research on the different facets of mindfulness is also beneficial because of the clear, intelligible descriptions it produces, which make it easier to explain mindfulness to patients.

How Does Mindfulness Work?

Scientific research into the functional mechanisms behind mindfulness is fairly recent. A detailed discussion of various explanatory models is provided by Baer (2010), who lists mindfulness, decentering, psychological flexibility, values, emotion regulation, self-compassion, spirituality, brain change, and changes in attention and working memory as relevant factors.

- Mindfulness: Meditation exercises enhance awareness in daily life, which leads to enhanced well-being.
- Decentering: Thoughts are regarded as phenomena, which are not necessarily true or important; do not require personal investment; and do not call for any particular reaction.
- Psychological flexibility: Unpleasant and undesirable thoughts and feelings can be permitted to exist without coping in counterproductive ways, which allows one to act according to one's goals and values.
- Values: Becoming aware of important personal values and learning to act according to them.

- Emotion regulation: Noticing and permitting all emotions as they are experienced; not reacting automatically or on impulse, but in a rational and goal-oriented manner.
- Self-compassion: Being friendly to oneself, rather than condemning oneself; acknowledging that disappointment and painful feelings are part of human existence; staying mindful in challenging situations instead of running away or getting caught up.
- Brain change: Mindfulness leads to structural and functional changes in the brain that correspond to enhanced cognitive and emotional processing.
- Changes in attention and working memory: Improved attention capacity and working memory contribute to reduction of symptoms and greater psychological functioning.

In addition to the above, there are three other significant explanatory models: Interacting Cognitive Subsystems (ICS) theory, the Buddhist Psychological Model (BPM) of mindfulness, and therapeutic empathy.

Interacting Cognitive Subsystems (ICS) theory

The developers of MBCT (Teasdale et al., 1995) offer an explanation for the effects of mindfulness that is based on the information-processing model of Interacting Cognitive Subsystems (ICS). The model is predicated on multi-layered memory systems, in which all incoming stimuli, internal and external, are encoded in two ways: propositional ("knowing that…") and implicational ("feeling that…"). Propositional memory storage contains cognitions that can be expressed and understood linguistically. Implicational storage is more broad and can take the form of emotional experiences not directly expressible in language. At the implicational level, rational-based interventions like psychoeducation and the challenging of irrational thought become ineffectual. An oft-heard difficulty is that patients know what it is they should do, but that their feelings compel them to do otherwise. Rather than relying on verbal meaning

35

attributions at the propositional level, mindfulness interventions emphasize working with emotions at the implicational level (Baert, Goeleven, & Raedt, 2006).

The Buddhist Psychological Model (BPM) of mindfulness

Grabovac, Lau, and Willet (2011) have introduced an interesting conceptualization of mindfulness based on the Buddhist Psychological Model (BPM). The BPM is a stepwise description of the way in which our habitual reactions—that is, attachment to pleasant feelings and rejection of unpleasant feelings—lead to suffering. The stream of subjective experience is actually a rapid sequence of sensory impressions, feelings, and thoughts of which we are mostly unconscious. Each experience carries an immediate, spontaneous "feeling tone," which can be neutral, pleasant, or unpleasant, and which precedes all emotions, such as fear or anger, and their associated behavior. This process can be short-circuited in two ways: through mindfulness training and through insight. Increased mindfulness allows one to recognize dysfunctional processes more quickly, disengage attention from performing habitual emotional reactions, and focus on goal-driven behavior. Insight occurs when, through direct experience, one becomes aware of the three most fundamental attributes of existence, which are present throughout all experience: impermanence, suffering, and not-self.

- Impermanence: Sense impressions and mental events are transient (they arise and pass away)
- Suffering: Habitual reactions (i.e., attachment and aversion) to the feelings of a sense impression or mental event, and a lack of awareness of this process, lead to suffering.
- Not-self: Sense impressions and mental events do not contain or constitute any lasting, separate entity that could be called a self (Grabovac et al., 2011).

According to the BPM, the immediate, tangible, and repeated experience of these three interrelated qualities of existence leads to alleviation of psychological problems and improved psychological functioning. In the Buddhist tradition this eventually culminates in spiritual enlightenment.

Therapeutic empathy

The last few decades have seen an increased emphasis on protocol-based treatment, evidence-based medicine, and randomized clinical trials, all predicated on the assumption that the effectiveness of a treatment is fully or primarily afforded by specific therapeutic or psychopharmacological interventions. However, meta-analyses (e.g., Lambert & Barley, 2002; Wampold, 2001) have increasingly indicated that the effectiveness of therapy is due only in part to specific therapeutic techniques. Although many interventions seem relevant— or even crucial—in the treatment of particular disorders (e.g., exposure and response prevention for obsessive-compulsive disorder), their specific effects tend to be overestimated. The degree of influence of factors determining therapeutic success is estimated as follows: 15% therapeutic techniques, 40% extraneous factors (life situation, job, relationship, etc.), 15% placebo effects (positive expectations, faith), and 30% the therapeutic alliance and the therapist's personal qualities (Lambert & Barley 2001). The most positive features reported by patients when describing their interaction with therapists are empathic capacity, warmth, understanding, and acceptance, along with the absence of criticism, neglect, and rejection. These positive aspects are encapsulated in the term *empathy*. Empathy is an innate potential and a skill that can be developed.

Davidson et al. (2003) found that mindfulness meditation gave rise to brain activation in areas associated with compassion. Grepmair et al. (2007), using SCL-90 and other measures, evaluated the results of treatment provided by therapists in training, and found that therapists who meditated scored significantly higher than the nonmeditating control group. According to Lutz, Slagter, Dunne, and Davidson (2008), heightened awareness of one's bodily sensations and reactions is associated with increased empathy. A number of authors, such as

Fulton (2005, 2008), hold that a therapist's practice of mindfulness meditation cultivates not only empathy but other components of the therapeutic alliance as well. Benefits include increased attention in therapy, higher tolerance of patient emotions, greater acceptance, and a more open attitude.

The diversity of explanatory models of mindfulness complicates matters for practitioners and patients. There is a practical need for a straightforward explanatory model that is clear and compatible with existing knowledge about psychological interventions. An explanation on the basis of attention and emotion regulation satisfies these criteria.

Attention regulation as a functional mechanism

Attentional processes are in almost all cases pivotal in the processing of information and typically precede other types of processes in the brain. Dysfunctional attentional processes play a sizable role in many psychiatric conditions. How this works in anxiety and depression is described by Koster, Baert, and De Raedt (2006). People with a biological predisposition to anxiety disorders are excessively alert, which leads to: (a) elevated distractability in general; (b) increased scanning of the environment for threatening information; (c) selective attention to threatening information; (d) a broad field of attention prior to threat detection; (e) narrowed attention subsequent to threat detection. These attentional biases result in the world being experienced as an unsafe place. Moreover, such biases restrict attentional access to information that may contradict anxious expectations.

Similarly dysfunctional attentional processes play a role in depression. Information that confirms a somber outlook is more likely to be selected, negative memories are more likely to arise, and less attention is allocated to positive information. People with depression tend to place insufficient attention on positive experiences (McCabe & Toman, 2000), and people in somber moods are less likely to shift attention away from negative information than normal controls. In contrast, positive emotions correlate with more broad and open attention

(Fredrickson, 2004). Changes in the range of attention are linked to behavior change: broad and distributed attention corresponds to approach behavior, and narrowed attention to avoidance behavior (Förster, Friedman, Özelsel, & Denzler, 2006, Förster & Higgins, 2005).

For most people, attention is something you either have—to whatever degree—or you don't. It is something to be directed (active attention) or followed (passive attention). Yet attention is a complex phenomenon that has been studied by psychologists for over a hundred years. There are, in fact, several overlapping forms of attention: focused, sustained, selective, and divided attention. Training these capacities serves to enhance meta-awareness.

- Focused attention: Attending to one specific stimulus, activity, or task.
- Sustained attention: Attention maintained over an prolonged period of time.
- Selective or executive attention: The capacity to focus attention while simultaneously attending to relevant new information and ignoring irrelevant information.
- Divided attention: Alternating or sharing attention between multiple subjects or tasks, particularly routine activities.

These distinct attentional processes are inherently tied to the control and maintenance of desired behavior.

Training the aforementioned attentional processes serves to enhance meta-awareness. This is also referred to as metacognitive awareness, which relates specifically to cognition: knowing what one is thinking. The term meta-awareness, however, encompasses awareness of all that is experienced through thought and the senses. Meta-awareness means acting on manual pilot, rather than automatic pilot. Myriad terms have been put forward to identify this metaposition in the literature: disidentification, neutral observer, reperceiving, decentering, defusion, distancing, and impartial spectator (Smalley & Winston, 2010). Various studies support the notion that mindfulness works in part due to the augmentation of meta-awareness (Carmody, 2009;

Hargus, Crane, Barnhofer, & Williams 2010; Rapgay, Bystritsky, Dafter, & Spearman, 2011; Teasdale et al., 1995, 2000).

The brain responds to external and internal stimuli in different ways. One way is known as bottom-up (or stimulus-driven attention) in which the flow of attention is directed by stimulus features, such as when an unexpected sound or pain automatically and involuntarily draws our attention. The other way is top-down, also known as goal-driven or executive attention, which is controlled by the individual. The bottom-up processes involve areas of the brain that are, in evolutionary terms, as old as the brainstem. Top-down attention involves control mechanisms associated with newer areas of the brain, such as the frontal cortex (Posner & Petersen, 1990; Posner & Rothbart, 1998).

Top-down processes are also linked to working memory, which functions optimally when the "noise" surrounding stimuli, such as emotions, is effectively regulated. Working memory is a limited-capacity system that, in order to operate efficiently, relies on the filtering of nonrelevant information, thereby allowing new information into the system. Working memory is enhanced by mindfulness (Chiesa, Calati, & Serretti, 2011) and thus improves the ability to handle emotions.

Onraedt, Koster, Geraerts, de Lissnyder, and de Raedt (2011) pose that dysfunctional working memory processes form a risk factor for depression. Difficulties ignoring and eliminating negative information from working memory keep people with depression stuck in a vicious cycle of negative thoughts and emotions. Training attention, particularly selective and divided attention, is therefore of particular significance. Siegle, Ghinassi, and Thase (2007) found support for the benefits of training working memory in people with depression. There has also been research on optimal working memory loads in the treatment of post-traumatic stress disorder (PTSD). Mindful breathing and eye movements (Eye Movement Desensitization and Reprocessing; EMDR) while focusing on unpleasant thoughts, images, or bodily sensations, both resulted in similar reductions in the immediacy and emotional impact of negative experiences (Van den Hout et al., 2010).

Sustained mindfulness training allows one to better understand, recognize, and regulate one's attentional processes. This helps to gradually diminish one's tendency to automatically attend to and identify with particular thoughts or feelings, and frees up more attention and energy for a broader spectrum of experiences which would otherwise go unnoticed. Through repeated practice, this can become habit (Carmody, Baer, Lykins, & Olendzki, 2009).

Emotion regulation as a functional mechanism

Emotion plays a pivotal role in virtually all mental disorders. Emotions are complex phenomena comprising cognition, physiological responses, and behaviors associated with internal and external stimuli. They provide crucial information about internal and external events, motivate our actions, and communicate information to others. Emotion regulation is the process by which we influence which feelings we want to experience and when, how we experience them, and how they are expressed.

Recent perspectives on mental disorder, particularly Transdiagnostic Theory and Acceptance and Commitment Therapy, assume that emotion dysregulation lies at the core of all psychopathology (Farchione et al., 2012; Hayes, Wilson, Gifford, Follette, & Strosahl 1996; Watson, 2005). Regardless of the nature of their intense negative emotions, patients habitually tend to rely on the same dysfunctional strategies, such as avoidance, repression, and rumination. Although these have some effect in the short term, they exacerbate conditions in the long term. This offers an explanation for comorbodity as well as the fact that treatment effects can generalize from one disorder to another (Barlow et al., 2011).

Mindfulness-based interventions differ from standard cognitive-behavioral therapies and other treatment models in a very important way: Rather than attempting to change emotions and/or thought content, mindfulness entails tolerance. Meditation teaches one to notice distractions but not to engage them. As emotions represent the most challenging form of distraction, mindfulness involves continual confrontation with unpleasant feelings in the body and thoughts in the mind. Furthermore, heightened awareness also leads to greater insight into information regarding underlying factors (i.e., emotional awareness), such as the causes of emotions and their connection to unpleasant memories of past experience. In other words, mindfulness works like exposure. Goleman (1988) therefore refers to the result of mindfulness as "global desensitization." MBCT includes specific mindfulness exercises focusing on emotions, such as the Working with Difficulty Meditation (Segal et al., 2013).

Support for emotional regulation as the most significant functional mechanism in mindfulness can be found in Chambers, Gullone, and Allen (2009), Hill and Updegraff (2012), Rapgay et al. (2011, 2013), and Treanor (2011). Chiesa, Serretti, and Jakobsen (2013) offer a detailed description of structures and processes in the brain that are associated with mindfulness-based emotion regulation. Some researchers consider mindfulness a top-down process, while others consider it a bottom-up emotion regulation strategy. The hypothesis best supported by brain research is that, for beginning meditators, the benefits of mindfulness occur through top-down regulation from the prefrontal context to the limbic system. As meditators become more experienced, bottom-up processes acquire a greater role. Although there is a gradual shift from top-down to bottom-up processes, each continues to serve an important role in emotion regulation (Chiesa et al., 2013).

Summary

The fact that mindfulness works because it trains attention and emotion regulation provides a useful rationale for both practitioners and patients. It can be easily explained to patients using everyday examples or problematic events from the patient's own lived experience. Emotional problems always involve some activating event, followed by unpleasant or painful feelings, which then result in a critical response: "This is uncomfortable," "I don't want this," "this needs to stop." This in turn leads to countermeasures, such as particular modes of thinking and behaving, which are intended to resolve unpleasant bodily sensations and thoughts.

Mindfulness training enables one to recognize this pattern sooner and to maintain goal-driven attention without impulsive or automatic reactions. One learns to observe one's actions and situations as if from a distance, which provides not only insight but also the room and freedom to respond in different, more appropriate ways. Mindfulness training also develops one's ability to recognize distractions and let them go. As emotions are the most challenging of distractions, meditation provides a continuous learning process through which one acquires the flexibility to deal with problematic thoughts and bodily sensations. The combined training of attention and emotion regulation leads to a reduction of psychiatric symptoms and to improved health.

Part II
Training Manual

4

Framework

This training protocol covers eight group sessions of 90 minutes' duration, plus two follow-up sessions. Groups consist of 8 to 12 men and women between 18 and 65 years of age. While the composition of the group may vary, an attempt should be made to match participants. When a man signs up, for example, it would be appropriate to include another male in the group. Although this is not technically group therapy, we still subscribe to the "Noah's Ark principle" of "two of every kind," since validation, recognition, and learning capacity are enhanced when participants can identify with other group members. A particular group may contain impulsive individuals who quickly and regularly display emotions, as well as inhibited and detached subjects with blunted or flat affect. The underlying idea of a varied group is that, in a safe training environment, everyone can learn from each other.

The main feature setting a training protocol apart from a treatment protocol is that everything discussed in the group relates to the acquisition of skills. While there is some room for participants' insights,

Mindfulness and Schema Therapy: A Practical Guide, First Edition.
Michiel van Vreeswijk, Jenny Broersen and Ger Schurink.
© 2014 John Wiley & Sons, Ltd. Published 2014 by John Wiley & Sons, Ltd.

these are ideally linked back to the training. Group dynamics, to the extent they are present, are utilized for illustrating the interactions between automatic pilot and schemas/modes. The trainer's attitude is one of curiosity and openness to whatever participants bring to the table, through which they effectively model the desired mindfulness-based approach to experience. Additionally, trainers provide psychoeducation concerning schemas, modes, and schema coping.

Another distinction between this training protocol and those prescribed by, for example, Segal et al. (2002), is that trainers are expected to fulfill a more action-oriented and regulating function, entailing a greater degree of psychoeducation. This manner of training has been found to be indispensable when training individuals with more serious personality problems, making the trainers' task all the more challenging; thus, trainers need to be mindfully action-oriented.

Instead of delving into participants' personality problems at large, three of each group member's most influential schemas and modes are identified, which then function as the object of attention over the course of the training. By concentrating the focus on these specific schemas and modes, awareness and understanding of schema processes are facilitated.

The first two sessions revolve around the description, explanation, and practice of basic mindfulness skills. Exercises include those described in mindfulness-based cognitive therapy for depression (Segal et al., 2002), among others. In the third session, participants practice mindful awareness of painful memories. From session 4 onwards, participants learn to consciously observe their schemas and modes in action. In sessions 5 and 6, participants are also asked to challenge their schemas on a cognitive level, practicing the mindfulness-based doing mode. Sessions 7 and 8 involve exercises that facilitate mindful awareness of the Healthy Adult and Happy Child modes. In conclusion, two follow-up sessions will be planned, offering the opportunity for participants to refresh their memories and learn additional mindfulness exercises in the context of schemas and modes.

Our descriptions of mindfulness exercises intentionally incorporate an explicit distinction between the attention-oriented aspect and the action-oriented aspect (doing mode) of an exercise. This division is not intended to create an artificial division between the two, but rather to help participants become aware of these as dual processes.

At the following website, http://www.mfvanvreeswijk.com, patients can buy mindfulness exercises (audio files), like the ones in this book. We consider these required listening, as experience has shown the training to be more effective when participants practice on their own, outside of the group meetings.

Pre- and post-measures of the training are obtained with the aid of questionnaires (YSQ and SMI-1), in which participants record their experiences. One of the questionnaires is administered multiple times over a number of sessions (Five Facet M Questionnaire, Baer, 2010). Results are returned to participants, providing them with additional insight into their experiences during the training. Note that the terms employed in these questionnaires reflect a focus on experience, rather than outcome effect. Any mention of effects will elicit the notion that training is expected to bring about some kind of change in symptoms, schemas, or modes. Although change may certainly occur, it is not the objective. The aim of the training is to learn to be mindful, without action-orientedness, and without preconceived goals.

5

(Contra)indications

A fairly anxious young man with symptoms of melancholy has signed up for an initial assessment. The patient has withdrawn from school and spends most of his time sitting at home, playing video games or brooding in front of the TV. He had a history of dropping out of previous therapies before completion. The patient's prominent schemas are Failure, Emotional Deprivation, and Social Isolation, and his most frequently active modes include Detached Protector, Vulnerable Child, and Demanding Parent. He truly wants to be helped and is ready to do the work, but fears he will end up dropping out again.

The patient agrees to follow eight sessions of the training Mindfulness and Schema Therapy, prior to starting therapy. This offers him the prospect of actually completing a therapy treatment program for a change. The relatively brief training period will also provide an introduction to Schema Therapy,

Mindfulness and Schema Therapy: A Practical Guide, First Edition.
Michiel van Vreeswijk, Jenny Broersen and Ger Schurink.
© 2014 John Wiley & Sons, Ltd. Published 2014 by John Wiley & Sons, Ltd.

enabling him to determine whether or not he is sufficiently motivated to continue therapy and to do the homework which would be required. It also presents him with an alternative to withdrawal and rumination, avoiding the ever-present distraction of video games and TV.

Mindfulness training is increasingly used in clinical settings with a variety of patient demographics, however, effectiveness studies lag behind. So far, there are no scientifically supported criteria for indications and contraindications. In this protocol, criteria are based on insights from the authors' clinical experience, and the guidelines for psychotherapy and psychological treatment in general.

Indication criteria are:

- openness to becoming aware of habitual patterns (schemas/modes);
- recurring Axis I disorders involving apparent personality disorder/ problems;
- persistent rumination;
- difficulties regulating emotion;
- impulsivity, and a preparedness to examine and change it;
- recurring difficulties in social interaction;
- openness to Schema Therapy, albeit with uncertainty regarding long-term Schema Therapy treatment;
- openness to Schema Therapy, albeit with limited insight into schemas and modes (e.g. as indicated by unexpectedly low scores on questionnaires).

Contraindications include:

- overly severe Axis I disorders, where patients are unable to adequately concentrate on exercises, or where exercises appear overly taxing from the very start (e.g. in cases of severe substance abuse disorder);

- severe learning disability;
- unpreparedness to invest time in mindfulness exercises;
- unpreparedness to plan predetermined actions for crisis situations;
- socioeconomic living circumstances requiring immediate attention (e.g. pending eviction, overwhelming financial debt, legal actions);
- lack of support for participation in the training in patient's social network;
- lack of proficiency in the spoken language.

Specific contraindications for group-based mindfulness training are:

- lack of empathic capacity;
- hearing deficiencies.

6

Training

Diagnostics, Initial Assessment, and Effect Measures

The patient completes a number of questionnaires preceding the initial assessment. The therapist sends these out a couple of weeks in advance, so that results can be discussed in the first meeting.

The following questionnaires are administered:

- Brief Symptom Inventory (BSI; Derogatis & Spencer, 1982);
- Young Schema Questionnaire (YSQ-2; Schmidt et al., 1995);
- Schema Mode Inventory-1 (SMI-1; Lobbestael et al., 2007).

The questionnaires are scored prior to the initial assessment. The results are used to determine the three highest-scoring schemas and modes. These are listed in a report (see Appendix II-A for an example), issued to the patient at the initial assessment. Analysis of the patient's

Mindfulness and Schema Therapy: A Practical Guide, First Edition.
Michiel van Vreeswijk, Jenny Broersen and Ger Schurink.
© 2014 John Wiley & Sons, Ltd. Published 2014 by John Wiley & Sons, Ltd.

file and conversations with referring parties can also supply useful information to supplement the assessment.

In the initial assessment, it is explained to the patient that the questionnaires form part of the training: they are administered at initiation and conclusion of the treatment program, and are also used to identify the patient's three highest-scoring schemas and modes. Setting up a meeting for an initial assessment is conditional upon completion of the questionnaires. Although most patients do complete and hand in the material on time, some do not. If a patient with the schema Insufficient Self-Control/Self-Discipline accordingly fails to fill in the questionnaires, then the patient and therapist can collaborate on making a behavioral analysis. The patient is informed that the training Mindfulness and Schema Therapy involves a lot of exercises and assignments, and that it is important to carry these out. The patient should be aware that the amount of effort put into his questionnaires functions as an indicator of his future motivation to perform mindfulness exercises.

Interpretations of questionnaire results should preferably be written on a whiteboard. The patient's three highest-scoring schemas and modes are discussed, along with his three highest-scoring psychological symptoms. An exploration of the patient's experiences in daily life should yield examples that illustrate the functioning of his schemas and modes. Effort should be made to assess the patient's capacity for recognizing when his symptoms increase, and to evaluate his comprehension of the role of "automatic pilot" in such situations (e.g. automatic ways of reaction in that specific situation). It is important to ascertain whether this patient has a tendency toward impulsivity, or does he demonstrate inhibition and excessive control? Does he interpret his symptoms as signs of weakness? On the basis of the patient's three predominant schemas and modes, the functioning of his "automatic pilot" is gradually brought to light.

Following the assessment, the therapist provides some information about the training:

Much of what we do, we do on automatic pilot. The way your automatic pilot shapes your response to situations, involving yourself and others, is greatly influenced by schemas and modes. For instance, when the Unrelenting Standards schema is triggered, you might respond to the feelings of restlessness by working very hard, setting exceptionally high standards for yourself. When you see someone get upset, you might go out of your way to take care of that person, losing sight of your personal boundaries in the process (Compliant Surrender mode)—or you could detach and merely feign interest (Detached Protector mode). We all have different ways of dealing with our situations and emotions, and we tend to stick to the same strategies. However, always depending on the same reactions comes with certain disadvantages, not least of which is the development of tunnel vision. Tunnel vision makes it difficult to see alternative ways of thinking, acting, and feeling.

The training Mindfulness and Schema Therapy teaches you to recognize when schemas and modes are triggered. You learn to monitor schemas, emotions, and behavior without acting on them automatically. The training will require a very open and broad interest in your experience. You will become aware that thoughts, emotions, and behavior are experiences that come and go, each following their natural course. Sometimes your experiences intensify, and sometimes they subside. Either way, they always follow a predictable pattern of coming and going, just like the tide.

During the eight weeks of training, you will spend of lot of time writing in your workbook and practicing mindfulness exercises. It might not be easy. Some people are highly impulsive, which makes it hard for them to practice; they find the exercises boring or tedious, or they don't plan for them in their agendas. Others, operating from the Unrelenting Standards schema, expect immediate results, getting frustrated when solutions aren't handed to them immediately. Some people reduce their practice when they get depressed, anxious, or ruminative, while others practice less when things seem to be going just fine. Let's find out what kind of pitfalls you may encounter during the exercises practiced over the course of this training. We want to learn how you deal with situations, thoughts, emotions, actions, and physical sensations when you're on automatic pilot.

If the patient indicates an interest in participating, then further practical considerations are discussed. The composition and rules of the group are laid out, including confidentiality and expectations of punctuality. Information is provided about training fees as well as trainer contact information. The patient receives a leaflet about the mindfulness training (see Appendix II-B).

The patient should understand that learning to recognize their own "automatic pilot" does not in itself mean that symptoms will decline or that an all-encompassing solution has been found. It is explained that increased awareness of engrained patterns can help to expand the patient's perspective of situations, thoughts, emotions, and behavior; that mindfulness decreases the effect of tunnel vision.

The results from questionnaires, the patient file analysis, and the initial assessment will be used to predict possible pitfalls the patient may encounter during training. Someone with the schema Unrelenting Standards is likely to be impatient for results, desiring to know the objective of every exercise in advance. Someone scoring high on the Undisciplined Child mode will have trouble practicing the exercises on a regular basis, and will find them boring. These behaviors are linked back to their own "automatic pilot." Exploring such potential barriers to progress in the context of the training can increase the patient's motivation to perform exercises, and will make it easier to address automatic patterns and deal with them as they arise.

Martha presents with rapid mood swings. She shows a tendency to become hostile toward others when they get too close and personal. Whenever Martha feels down, she tends to withdraw.

During the initial assessment, Martha's automatic responses are connected to her Abandonment/Instability schema. Possible reactions to the mindfulness training are hypothesized, including potential urges to withdraw from the group, avoid contributing, present an inflated image of herself, or to claim that she can manage well enough on her own. Martha acknowledges these as real possibilities, and consents that the trainers may point out her automatic pilot whenever it is engaged.

Patients are asked to complete the Five-Facet M Questionnaire (Appendix III-B; Baer, 2010) during sessions 1, 3, 5, and 7. This self-report measures the frequency of everyday mindfulness experiences. It is used to help participants attain new perspectives of themselves. The questionnaire requires that they look at their results with mindfulness, without falling into action-oriented patterns. Without immediately thinking: "How can I improve? What needs to change?"

Following the last session, participants retake the BSI, YSQ, and SMI-1 tests. The results are scored, documented in a report, and compared with pre-training scores. The combined results are all discussed with the participant, and any conclusions provide a basis for determining whether to conclude the program, or proceed with continued treatment.

Training Attitude

Intimacy, warmth, support, interest, and respect are some of the qualities that trainers can bring to the training with positive effect. Throughout the training, trainers should continually focus on attitude, rather than experience. There is a shift in emphasis from the content of experience to the orientation toward experience. Participants feel validated when trainers approach them with an inviting, attentive, and curious attitude. Aim to inquire about their experiences after every exercise, making sure to follow up on their answers with further questioning. What sort of physical sensations, thoughts, and feelings did they experience, and what were they like? What meaning did they ascribe to their experiences? The trainer's curiosity can help to stimulate participants' own interest in their personal experiences.

We recommend that one of the trainers join the group during mindfulness exercises, keeping his eyes closed and maintaining an upright and dignified posture. In doing so, the trainer becomes a role model for participants, who will frequently become anxious or upset at the idea of being watched as they practice. Furthermore, participants should feel free to pick any spot or position in the training environment to carry out their exercises. They may sit in a corner or turn their back toward the group, if that is what they feel most comfortable with. The important thing is for participants to feel uninhibited and at ease during their exercises, and not to become preoccupied with worrying about their environment.

Segal, Teasdale, and Williams (2002) advise trainers to become adept at mindfulness themselves, before attempting to instruct others. Trainers should have made mindfulness exercises a daily habit, developing their understanding of the principles of mindfulness from an "inside perspective." When Segal et al. carried out their pilot training, it became clear that sole instruction by pre-recorded mindfulness audio files and homework assignments was not effective. Trainers are more capable of handling problems that participants encounter during the training when they themselves are experienced with the material. A purely intellectual understanding will not suffice; trainers should be able to use their own words and actions to convey the attitudes and techniques that mindfulness involves. Segal et al. make an analogy with swimming lessons: a competent instructor is a good swimmer and practices regularly.

Sessions should allow plenty of time for discussion after exercises. There won't be enough time to address all participants and their experiences, so trainers will want to focus on a different person's homework for each new session.

Post-exercise discussions require a training attitude that is attentive, inviting, and inquisitive. Our experience has shown that each participant will respond differently to exercises, so be sure to question them with a curious yet considerate attitude. What did you experience during your exercises? Were there moments in your day when you thought of practicing an exercise? What went through your mind as you decided to postpone your practice? Try to determine any potential schemas and modes involved in their exercise practice.

A 27-year-old man named Bert has just started mindfulness training. He began seeing a therapist because his Demanding Parent mode is a source of problems in his life. He has been floundering at work, and his Demanding Parent mode routinely makes him feel bad. He used to take care of things quickly and efficiently, but lately he has been putting them off or avoiding them altogether.

At the second training session, Bert tells the trainer that he's having trouble with his exercises. Upon further inquiry, the trainer learns that Bert has been practicing, but he's struggling to stay focused and see his exercises through till the end. When asked about his feelings and physical sensations while practicing, Bert says that his body becomes restless, and that he feels impatient and annoyed. He would rather just get up, stop listening to the audio file, and go and do something worthwhile. Nevertheless, he decided to complete his exercises and practice them four times a week. The trainer writes down all of Bert's thoughts, feelings, and physical sensations on a whiteboard. Normally, Bert doesn't pay this much attention to his experience. He's accustomed to just acting on his experiences, as if directed by "automatic pilot." But now that his experiences are plainly visible for him to see, Bert realizes that he can be quite self-demanding, and that he is quick to judge himself. This is a recurring pattern.

In the above example, the trainer's inquisitive approach and follow-up questions lead Bert to understand that he has, in fact, become aware of several patterns of thoughts and urges during his mindfulness exercises. Becoming aware of those experiences is pivotal.

When a participant's account of his mindfulness experiences is lacking in bodily sensations, feelings, and/or thoughts, be sure to question him about these:

> Bert explains that he keeps feeling resistance and irritation during his mindfulness exercises. This occurs quite frequently. The trainer asks Bert if he can locate this feeling of resistance in his body. He answers that there is some tension in his stomach. When invited to pay closer attention to that physical sensation, to allow the experience, Bert's resistance starts to fade. He gradually becomes aware of feelings of sadness and despair. These are feelings Bert has never been able to tolerate well.

Participants sometimes doubt the usefulness of homework assignments. Listen attentively to their doubts, and enquire further. Try and identify when a participant is responding on automatic pilot.

> Bert remarks that he finds it difficult to wind down and get some rest. How can he be expected to settle down and meditate in such a busy, frenetic society? The trainer responds that it may not be a matter of settling down. The important thing is to act with attention, with mindfulness. The trainer offers the following illustration: "It's like you're on a hunting trip, running around chasing your prey. Frantically firing in all directions, hoping to hit a target. What would happen if you actually tried focusing on your prey?" A participant responds: "You would probably aim before firing, and you'd be more likely to hit your target."

Bert's example shows that not all participants enjoy these exercises. Their dissatisfaction may be a factor of particular schemas or modes. The Unrelenting Standards/Hypocritical schema can lead someone to restrict the time they allow themselves for practice. Experience suggests that individuals with the Insufficient Self-Control/Self-Discipline schema tend to become bored with mindfulness exercises. Work together with participants to uncover the way schemas influence their performance and experience of the homework assignments.

It is important for trainers to record all of the group's experiences on a whiteboard or notebook. Providing an overview of what has been voiced about exercises makes it easier for participants to follow discussions, respond to one another, and pose questions. Writing things down is also supportive of an inquisitive and curious approach. It is not practical to write all of each session's experiences down; doing so for just one exercise should suffice.

The Training Program

The training consists of eight sessions and two follow-up sessions, and is designed for a group setting. Sessions take place once a week and last one and a half hours.

The structure of each session is pretty much the same. Starting from session 2, participants give up their notebook upon arrival. The sheets are used to rate schema mindfulness scores on a weekly basis, graded on a scale from 0 to 10 (0 = schema not at all mindfully observed, 10 = schema observed with full mindfulness). See Appendix II-C for an example. From session 2 onwards, a brief mindfulness exercise is performed prior to discussion of the homework assignments. Each session comprises one or more extended mindfulness exercises. New exercises are given out as homework. Sessions are concluded with another brief mindfulness exercise.

The training can also be delivered on an individual basis. Individual sessions usually last less than 90 minutes. Completing the entire program in each sitting, as described for the group format, is not feasible.

Individual sessions start with a brief mindfulness exercise, then cover the weekly schema mindfulness ratings as recorded in their notebook. Allow plenty of time for discussing homework assignments.

The training program is thoroughly described below. The mindfulness exercises practiced during sessions and assigned as homework are fully catalogued in Part III of this book (Participant Workbook), in which every exercise and its theoretical background are explained. Trainers are advised to read this information in advance and to refer to it in every session.

Session 1: Schemas, Modes, and Mindfulness Training

Program

- Introduction: After an opening talk, the participants briefly introduce themselves. Ask about previous experience with mindfulness exercises. You can also inquire about any yoga or meditation experience.
- Explanation of schemas and modes: Discuss the objective of mindfulness training.
- Raisin exercise: Let the group perform the exercise, and follow up with a discussion. Ask participants to share their experiences, and write their accounts on a whiteboard. Afterwards, explain the objective of this exercise.
- Schemas and modes notebook: Instruct participants to write their three highest-scoring schemas and modes in their notebook (see Appendix II-C for an example), which are then put up on a wall. Every week (starting from session 2), the participants will be asked to rate the degree of mindfulness with which each of their schemas was observed (0 = schema not at all mindfully observed, 10 = schema observed with full mindfulness). Ask them to bring their sheets to all future sessions.
- Body Scan exercise: Acquaint the group with the exercise instructions. Let the group practice for a while, after which members can relate their experiences. Record these on a whiteboard. Trainers should

endeavor to maintain a nonjudgmental attitude during the discussion, following up participant experiences with further questioning.

• Homework: Discuss the homework for the following session. Show participants how to fill in their assigned homework forms.

Homework explanation: Everyday Mindfulness

The exercise covered in today's session is a great technique for practicing mindfulness in your day-to-day life (see Appendix III-C). All you need to do is pick one of your daily activities or chores, and go through it with focused attention. Try practicing mindfulness while brushing your teeth, blow-drying your hair, or taking a shower. You can use this exercise in social situations, or in the company of loved ones. Some examples include: a mindful conversation over a meal with your partner, or talking to your mother on the phone. The key here is to focus your attention on the activity, and specifically on the experience. If you're brushing your teeth, pay attention to the way the brush feels against your teeth, or how your toothpaste tastes. Sense the movement of the brush inside your mouth. Just make sure to notice whenever your thoughts trail off, so you can re-focus on the activity at hand. Once you start taking in the full experience of these little moments in your life, it gets easier to become aware of your automatic pilot (Segal et al., 2006).

Questionnaire explanation: Five Facet M Questionnaire (see Appendix III-C)

This questionnaire (Baer, 2010) measures the frequency of everyday mindfulness experiences. The list contains 39 items, each of which can be rated on a 5-point scale of experience (1 = never or very rarely true, 5 = very often or always true).

You'll be asked to fill in this questionnaire at sessions 1, 3, 5, and 7. At the end of every session, take a moment to look at your scores. Do you notice anything? You don't have to see any changes or results. Just focus on your objective, which is to observe without judgment and without action.

Homework explanation: Becoming Aware of your Schemas

This training teaches you to become aware of the activation of your schemas, and to recognize which ones are being triggered. A useful strategy is to keep track of the number of times per week when you notice your top three schemas in action. For this exercise, you can use the Personal Mindfulness Evaluation forms, which should be filled in before the start of every session. That way each of your top three schemas receives attention on a regular basis.

Homework assignment: Writing a Summary

You will receive a lot of information from trainers and group members in this training. A popular technique for remembering information is to write it down in your own words. You can do this using the "Writing a Summary" form (see Appendix III-D). Each session's summary will include the number of sessions attended to date, the number of sessions still available, a brief description of the current session, a summary of what you've learned this session, what you wish to retain, and your homework for the following session. Keeping a record of what you have learned will improve your recall and expand your benefit from the training. When in need of a refresher, you can refer to information from your own notebook, relevant to your personal experience.

Session 2: Mindfulness of Your Environment

Program

- Schema and mode notebooks: Participants rate their level of schema mindfulness over the past week (see session one). If participants forget to bring their notebook with them, have them write up new ones (the same applies in subsequent sessions).

- Brief Body Scan meditation (5 minutes): The trainer can reference the body scan explanation from session one.
- Discussion of mindfulness scores and homework assignments: Ask if the group managed to practice the body scan at home. If so, let one of the trainers write the group's experiences and insights on a whiteboard. Now that these experiences have been described and written down, what do the participants notice? Are there any discernible patterns to these experiences? A participant might notice, for instance, an emphasis on mental experiences and a lack of physical and emotional observations. In which case, the trainer can inquire about those missing aspects.

  If a participant hasn't practiced, follow up on that. Examine any possible events or thoughts that prevented the participant from practicing, and write these on the board. Explore their reasons in a nonjudgmental way, making clear to participants that doing the homework is not the goal. The goal is to become mindful of whatever happens before and during each exercise. Not to achieve transformations or results, but to grow in awareness.
- Everyday Mindfulness exercise: Which daily activities did the group select? Did participants stick to one thing or alternate between multiple activities? If the latter, what made them decide to mix it up? Ask about any distractions or disturbances that occurred during the exercise. Which thoughts played a role in sidetracking their attention? Explore the various emotions and bodily sensations that participants observed. Be sure to follow up on answers, always doing your best to react in nonjudgmental ways. It doesn't matter how or if participants did their homework, as long as they make an effort to become aware of anything that may have interfered. Again: the goal is awareness, not results.
- Mindfulness of Your Environment exercise: Practice this exercise in the group. Afterwards, discuss experiences and record any observations on the board.
- Homework: Conclude this session with next week's homework assignment.

Session 3: Mindful Breathing

Program

- Schema and mode notebooks: Participants rate their level of schema mindfulness over the past week.
- Three Minute Breathing Space exercise: Explain how the breath can be employed as a practical aid to concentration.
- Discussion of schema mindfulness scores and homework assignments: Were participants able to complete the body scan exercises on the audio file? Inquire about the group's experiences, including those members who didn't practice, and explore any interfering factors. In the same way, cover the Mindfulness of Your Environment exercise from the audio file, and discuss the Everyday Mindfulness assignment. All discussions can explore the role of schemas and modes in dealing with homework.
- Mindfulness of Painful Memories exercise: Practice this exercise in the group. Let participants discuss their experiences and record their observations on a whiteboard.
- Mindful Walking: Explain the instructions for this exercise. Trainers should make sure participants understand the exercise before taking them outdoors, if so desired. In the group discussion that follows, record all thoughts, actions, feelings, and/or physical experiences on the whiteboard.
- Conclusion: Assign the homework for the following session, and finish up with the Three Minute Breathing Space exercise.

Session 4: Mindfulness of Schema Coping

Program

- Schema and mode notebooks: Participants rate their level of schema mindfulness over the past week.

- Three Minute Breathing Space exercise: Explain how the breath can be employed as a practical aid to concentration.
- Discussion of schema mindfulness scores and homework assignments: Were participants able to perform the exercises from the audio files. If not, examine the thought patterns that may have impeded their efforts. Was the Mindfulness of Painful Memories exercise practiced? How about the Everyday Mindfulness exercise? Discuss experiences and investigate the appearance of recurring thought patterns. Are there particular schemas and modes that continue to arise before and during exercises?
- Schema coping: The concept of schema coping is explained by the trainers. Participants subsequently fill in the Schema Coping Questionnaire (see Participant Workbook) and calculate their scores. The results are then discussed in the group; do they reflect members' opinions of themselves?
- Mindful juggling: Each participant is allotted three small balls for juggling. Note: begin the exercise with just two balls. One trainer provides instructions and participates in the exercise, while the other monitors. If a group member is seen juggling two balls with little to no effort, hand him a third ball. After a minute or two give all participants another ball and a little later another one and so forth. Some patients stop instantly when they get a third or fourth ball, others try to keep going no matter how many balls they get and how many times the balls are dropping to the ground. The exercise is followed by a discussion on which schemas and modes were activated and when and what kind of schema coping was activated. Record experiences on the whiteboard.
- Conclusion: Discuss the homework for next week. Note: two new exercises on the audio files will be handed out. These have not yet been practiced in the group, but participants can read about them in the Participant Workbook. Assign the exercises for next week, and conclude the session with a Three Minute Breathing Space exercise.

Session 5: Allowing and Accepting What Is

Program

- Schema and mode notebooks: Participants rate their level of schema mindfulness over the past week.
- Three Minute Breathing Space exercise: Explain how the breath can be employed as a practical aid to concentration.
- Discussion of schema mindfulness scores and homework assignments: Where applicable, identify behavior indicating schema avoidance, schema compensation, and schema surrender. Ask whether participants have listened to and practiced the exercises on the audio files, including the two latest items (Become More Aware of Your Schemas, Get to Know Your Schemas Better). Do certain schemas get activated before and/or during the exercises?
- Three Minute Schema Mindfulness: Lead the group in this exercise. Write down and discuss participant experiences.
- Mindful Acceptance of Self and Other: The concept is explained by the trainers. Ask participants to read the text before beginning the exercise. The group is then divided into smaller groups, and members spend 20 minutes formulating acceptance-based thoughts regarding their schemas (see Participant Workbook, session 5). Emphasize how group members can help each other come up with positive and accepting thoughts. The results are discussed within each subgroup, and then integrated in a larger group discussion.
- Conclusion: Assign the homework for the following session, and finish up with the Three Minute Breathing Space exercise.

Session 6: Schemas: Fact or Fiction?

Program

- Schema and mode notebooks: Participants rate their level of schema mindfulness over the past week.

- Three Minute Breathing Space exercise: Explain how the breath can be employed as a practical aid to concentration.
- Discussion of schema mindfulness scores and homework assignments: When schemas seem to have been more active than usual, try to connect them to the content of last week's session. See if participants were able to monitor the triggering of their schemas with a more accepting attitude. Ask if they have listened to the recorded exercises, including the latest item (Three Minutes of Schema Contemplation). Spend some time on the Everyday Mindfulness exercise if deemed necessary. Are there any noticeable patterns in behavior and/or thought?
- Manifesting intent: Explain the concept of intention. Have the participants carry out the Walking with Mindful Intention exercise, which should be performed outdoors. Afterwards, discuss the group's experiences and write them on the board.
- Letting Go of Schemas: let the group practice this exercise. Take time during the discussion to focus on experiences.
- Conclusion: Assign the homework for the following session, and finish up with the Three Minute Breathing Space exercise.

Session 7: Caring for Yourself through the Healthy Adult and the Happy Child

Program

- Schema and mode notebooks: Participants rate their level of schema mindfulness over the past week.
- Three Minute Breathing Space exercise: Explain how the breath can be employed as a practical aid to concentration.
- Discussion of schema mindfulness scores and homework assignments: Did participants experience any periods of schema mindfulness, without their automatic pilot? Inquire about Everyday Mindfulness and other audio files exercises. Did the group listen to the latest audio file exercise (Letting Go of Your Schemas)?

- Caring for Yourself through the Healthy Adult and the Happy Child: Explain the characteristics of these modes. The Mindfulness of the Healthy Adult and the Happy Child exercise is practiced and then discussed in the group. Write experiences on the whiteboard.
- Preparing for the Future: The trainers take five minutes to explain this exercise, then divide the group into smaller groups. Ask the members to read the related text in their workbooks before beginning the exercise. Remind them that they can help one another fill out the exercise sheets. Afterwards, gather the groups together and let them discuss their results.
- What Do the Healthy Adult and the Happy Child Need?: Explain this exercise to the group and set as homework.
- Mindfulness of Schemas as Mere Thoughts: Explain this exercise to the group and set as homework.
- Conclusion: Assign the homework for the following session, and finish up with the Three Minute Breathing Space exercise.

Session 8: The Future

Program

- Schema and mode notebooks: Homework forms are handed in and participants rate their level of schema mindfulness over the past week.
- Three Minute Breathing Space exercise: Explain how the breath can be employed as a practical aid to concentration.
- Discussion of schema mindfulness scores and homework assignments: Did participants manage to develop their awareness of the Healthy Adult and Happy Child? What kind of observations came up before or during this exercise?
- Mindful of Yourself as Child and Adult exercise: After explaining the concept of this exercise, let the group practice for a while. Discuss experiences and record them on the whiteboard.
- Juggling With Schema and Mode Mindfulness in Personal Interactions: Let the group perform the exercise in pairs. One trainer gives instructions while the other observes. Start with one ball for

each pair and then two, three and so forth. Tell the pairs that they are not allowed to talk to each other, but that they have to be mindfully aware of the other's needs by looking at how the other nonverbally responds to a thrown ball. After the exercise, in the discussion that follows, pay special attention to the role of schemas and modes in contact with the other person.

- Evaluation: Use the last 10 minutes of the session for an evaluation of the training program. Help participants understand how the mindfulness exercises learned can be applied on their own in the future. Also inform the group about the individual question-naire evaluations occurring at a later date. Some two weeks before the evaluation, questionnaires will be sent out. The results of these will be addressed during the evaluation session. Individual members will also be advised, where applicable, on any evident need for further treatment. Let the group know about the follow-up sessions. These group sessions will consist of the same members.

Follow-up Sessions

Let participants know there will be two follow-up sessions. The first follow-up takes place in one month's time, with the second session following two months later. At just one hour's length, follow-up sessions are shorter than regular meetings. The second session will include evaluation discussions with the participants.

The follow-up sessions are shorter than previous meetings due to the change in focus. Little time will be devoted to learning new skills and techniques. Instead, we will concentrate on retaining (and refreshing, if necessary) previously learned skills. Letting participants know about this change in emphasis will help them to prepare for the follow-up sessions. Participants should also be made aware that there will be little time for considering specific concerns. The follow-up sessions will primarily address the following questions: How have you been using mindfulness exercises as a way to develop schema and mode awareness? Which aspects of your practice have gone well over the past month, and which were more challenging? What do you intend to work on in the future? Have you considered how you will avoid falling back on the habit of responding to schemas and modes on automatic pilot?

Follow-up Session 1

The training program is limited to just eight sessions and two follow-up meetings. As such, it is not realistic to expect all of our participants to retain every learned skill and technique forever. That is why these follow-up sessions stress continued practice and maintenance of mindfulness skills. Our experience has shown that mindfulness exercises gradually become lost among one's other daily responsibilities, so the follow-up period will be used to establish strategies for maintaining, developing, and integrating mindfulness in everyday life. Participants will take home questionnaires to be filled in over the coming weeks. They will also be invited to individual evaluation meetings, which will take place in the second follow-up session.

Participants were informed in session 8 that the follow-up sessions will emphasize continued mindfulness development, rather than new skills and techniques to be learned. Remind the group that time to address specific concerns will be limited.

Program (1 hour)

- Schema and mode notebook: Participants write down scores indicating their degree of schema and mode mindfulness over the past month.
- Mindfulness exercise: The Healthy Adult Who Brings Mindfulness to Daily Life.
- Ask participants about their experiences with mindfulness since the last session.
- Divide into groups. Each group will think of concrete strategies for developing mindfulness and monitoring schemas/modes in the future. Groups can also come up with custom mindfulness-based

techniques. Each group will present a brief summary of its strategies and/or exercises.

- Provide each participant with a questionnaire and a return envelope.
  Ask them to mail the completed questionnaire after three weeks.
- Conclude the session with a Three Minute Mindfulness exercise.

Follow-up Session 2

Participants who are continuing in therapy can incorporate mindfulness exercises in individual therapy sessions as a way to maintain and
continue developing their skills after the training program has finished.
One possibility is to start and end every session with a Three Minute
Mindfulness exercise. Group instructors are also free to plan booster
training sessions for up to two years.

Today is the last official follow-up session. We will continue
working on strategies for future schema and mode mindfulness.
Participants will also meet with instructors for evaluations on an
individual basis.

Program (1 hour)

- Schema and mode notebook: Participants write down scores indicating their degree of schema and mode mindfulness over the past month.
- Group Mindfulness exercise: Choose one of the following exercises: (a) *The Healthy Adult Who monitors our Vulnerability, Responds
  with Gentleness, and has Hope for the Future,* or (b) *Planning a
  Mindful Future.* The exercise not chosen may be listened to and
  practiced at home.
- Ask participants about their experiences with mindfulness since
  the last session.
- Divide participants into groups. Groups will discuss their schema
  mindfulness progress and work on their strategies for future mindfulness. Each group will then present a brief summary.
- Bring the session to a close.

7

Pitfalls

Trainers and participants alike need to be mindful of pitfalls. After displaying schema mindfulness score sheets, each training session starts with a mindfulness exercise that facilitates a change from the action-oriented state of mind, to the attention-oriented state. This opening exercise is sometimes interrupted by latecomers knocking on the door. When this occurs, it is important for trainers to beware of lapsing back into action-orientedness. A common impulsive response among trainers is to go and open the door, thereby disrupting the mindfulness of the group. It is better for everyone present to remain seated and complete the exercise, even if the latecomer continues to knock. The trainer should mindfully identify the event as a mental distraction, one that urges toward an action-oriented state. If allowed to run its course, this distraction may trigger the trainer's Self-Sacrifice schema, evoking the idea that he should let the latecomer in; "it would be unkind to leave him waiting outside." Besides that, the Unrelenting Standards/Hypocritical schema might be activated, giving rise to judgmental thoughts like "the latecomer is inconveniencing the group," and "he should make more of an

Mindfulness and Schema Therapy: A Practical Guide, First Edition.
Michiel van Vreeswijk, Jenny Broersen and Ger Schurink.
© 2014 John Wiley & Sons, Ltd. Published 2014 by John Wiley & Sons, Ltd.

effort to arrive on time." Once the exercise is finished, the person can be let in, upon which a discussion may take place, emphasizing a nonjudgmental stance. Mindfully addressing the issue has a double effect: not only does it reaffirm the group's rule of starting and finishing on time, it also allows the trainer to illustrate how to deal with situations that tempt the mind to switch back to an action-oriented state.

A similar approach can be taken in regard to the session's conclusion. Participants often have a tendency to prepare their exit a few minutes prior to the session's end, so that they're ready to leave right away. The trainer can identify this action-orientedness and suggest that the session is concluded with a short mindfulness exercise. Participants can then choose to embark on the rest of their day from an attention-oriented state, without going into automatic pilot.

While the group discusses the homework for next week's session, Bernadette is already packing her bag. This creates a noticeable amount of noise. The trainer stops for a moment to address what is happening. He asks Bernadette what has caused her to start packing up. She explains that she has to leave on time to pick her kids up from school. Upon further questioning it becomes clear that, for the past half hour, her mind has been busy with all the things she needs to get done this afternoon. Besides picking up the kids, she has to get groceries, drop one of the kids off at soccer practice, and cook. The list goes on and on. After some more questioning, it eventually emerges that her schemas, Unrelenting Standards/Hypocritical and Self-Sacrifice, have been influencing her behavior during the training and at home. Bernadette rarely asks her partner for help, which means she carries most of the household responsibilities by herself.

The trainer asks whether Bernadette was aware that her thoughts were being sidetracked over the past half hour. She was not, nor was she aware of being in an action-oriented state. She now realizes that, by worrying about her considerable to-do list, she spent the better part of this session being action-oriented.

Participants sometimes forget to bring their notebook sheets containing their schema mindfulness scores. Ask these persons to grab a new sheet and rewrite their schemas and modes, along with their mindfulness scores. When a sheet has been forgotten, it may be pertinent to make a behavior analysis. Do this from a nonjudgmental and mindful stance. Take a moment to consider how this person managed to forget, and see if you can relate it to his schemas and modes. Does their lapse of memory have anything to do with the Insufficient Self-Control/Self-Discipline schema? Is the participant continually busy caring for others, so that he lacks the time to care for himself (Self-Sacrifice schema), causing him to forget his notebook?

> Evelyn has forgotten to bring the notebook with her schema mindfulness scores to the training. The trainers remark that this isn't the first time she has left her material at home. Evelyn explains how she's always in a hurry to get to the session on time. In fact, she ends up rushing to almost all of her appointments. Her Insufficient Self-Control/Self-Discipline schema frequently leads her to act on impulse. When questioned further, it emerges that Evelyn does not like feeling alone, and that is why she's always busy. When she stops to contemplate this pattern in her behavior, Evelyn realizes that she's constantly occupying herself, in order to escape from feeling lonely. She becomes aware of how tired and agitated she actually feels, and recognizes that her current lifestyle prevents her from taking adequate care of herself.

Participants are sometimes highly anxious at the idea of keeping their eyes closed during exercises. For example, the Mistrust and/or Abuse schema can cause individuals to worry about being abused by others while in a vulnerable state. These participants might feel safer knowing that one of the trainers is with them in this state of vulnerability, also with his eyes shut. Trainers should inform the group that members are allowed to look for their own ways to carry out exercises, so that they feel comfortable while practicing. Let them know that it's okay to keep their eyes open, if that's what they need. If so, advise these participants to concentrate on a specific spot in their field of vision.

For some participants, exercises performed in the group can bring up painful images and memories. Members who grew up in unsafe and unpredictable conditions may feel very threatened when asked to join in exercises where the goal is not stated in advance. Their Mistrust and/or Abuse schema may be activated, sometimes to such a degree that they find themselves unable to focus on Healthy Adult and/or Happy Child schemas. This inability may upset them. Take time with these individuals to consider what is happening inside them. Address them in an open, empathic, and inquisitive way. What sort of thoughts, emotions, and behaviors are they experiencing? What do they feel in their bodies? Invite them to continue the exercise with eyes open. When someone indicates that an exercise has given them too much to manage and they need to stop, show them understanding. Explain that an observation of something painful, or of being unable to identify the Healthy Adult or Happy Child within oneself, each represent an opportunity to continue observing with an open, curious perspective, without necessarily orienting oneself for action. In other words, now could be a time for mindfulness; action can wait till later.

Another pitfall involved in mindfulness exercises is the risk of falling asleep. Do not judge a participant for falling asleep, but explore what has led to his sleepiness. Is this person simply tired from lack of sleep, or is falling asleep a strategy for avoiding self-awareness? Explain that it is important to stay awake during this exercise. Sleep makes it impossible to monitor thoughts, feelings, and physical experience. In order to stay awake, suggest that the participant open his eyes and make small movements once in a while. Then refocus attention on the breath and on the exercise at hand.

Max regularly falls asleep during mindfulness exercises. The trainers have previously advised him on how to prevent this from happening. After some questioning, it appears that Max initially does try out their suggestions, but that his thoughts end up trailing off. At that point, he is no longer in control of his attention, drifting further into unawareness of his thoughts, feelings, and bodily sensations. When the trainers inquire about the subject of his distracting thoughts, Max replies that he fantasizes and daydreams about "everything under the sun," but he can't remember what exactly. When he starts paying attention to this pattern in his behavior, he gradually realizes how daydreaming, and the sleep that follows, allows him to escape the reality of his day-to-day life and feelings. As such, daydreaming becomes a way to comfort himself. It is his Detached Self-Soother mode at work.

Homework assignments can also come with pitfalls. After some attempts, participants may stop doing homework altogether. Look into this development when it occurs, and explore which schemas and modes might play a role. Some participants may feel that the training isn't yielding results as fast as they would like, and so they abandon any further efforts (Unrelenting Standards/ Hypocritical schema or Failure schema).

Although the Everyday Mindfulness exercise seems fairly straightforward, many participants have trouble with it. It is important to select only one routine activity, like brushing teeth, drinking tea, or eating lunch. Participants should preferably practice this exercise while alone and at a regular time of day.

Sometimes the Everyday Mindfulness exercise is not practiced, simply because the activity poses too much of a challenge. A participant with the Insufficient Self-Control/Self-Discipline schema might say that he will attend to his dirty dishes every day, but if dishwashing isn't a normal part of his daily routine, he is unlikely to start now. In other words, failure to complete the exercise is a predictable outcome. Although this failure could in turn become the subject of mindfulness, expecting too much from someone already unaccustomed to attention-oriented behavior is simply unrealistic.

Participants may also stop listening to exercise audio files after just one session, particularly if they are bothered by the tone or quality of the narrator's voice. Invite these participants to try listening to the audio files from an open and enquiring place, to pay attention to their own experience without jumping into action-mode. If the problem persists, start looking for alternatives. One option to consider is letting participants or their loved ones record their own narration of the material.

When group members fail to carry out their assignments, trainers can investigate whether or not schemas, modes, or schema coping have been of any influence. However, the group should be aware that schema avoidance, compensation, and surrender aren't necessarily maladaptive coping strategies in each and every case. What's important is to make a mindful selection from possible strategies for dealing with situations, emotions, and thoughts.

The same principle applies to participants who discontinue the body scan or other breath-centered mindfulness exercises. Some members of the group may notice that being mindful of their breathing produces feelings of anxiety. Explain that nothing about the breath needs to be changed. People often believe that they should breathe from the stomach. Help participants to recognize that the urge to escape from breath exercises usually reflects a tendency to escape from anything that feels unpleasant.

When despondent participants continue to feel hopeless throughout the training and, for example, keep wondering about the purpose of all these exercises, trainers may themselves begin to experience feelings of desperation, inadequacy, and failure, along with thoughts of self-blame and admonishments to try harder. Underlying such experiences is usually a need for efficiency and control (Unrelenting Standards/ Hypocritical schema). The fact is that participants are typically slow to adopt the rationale behind these exercises. They keep asking how these practices can help them, for instance, to better handle emotions, like sadness and anger, or the urge to cut, or recurring thoughts of death.

When these kind of questions arise, it is extra important for trainers to remain mindful by, for example, returning to the breath as a neutral anchor point. This provides the (experienced) trainer with more space to consider his possible responses. Oftentimes it will suffice to empathically and mindfully explore these participants' feelings of desperation, using a notebook write down exactly what it is they may be experiencing—in terms of thoughts, emotions, and behavior— and in what part of the body their feelings are most strongly felt. Do not enter into discussion about their observations or challenge their thoughts and feelings. Simply explore what it is they notice about them. Endeavor to respond with renewed attention whenever a partici-pant brings up his doubts or feelings of despair, as if for the first time. Examine the activity of modes, such as the Vulnerable Child, Demanding Parent, and/or Punitive Parent. When a trainer succeeds in remaining empathic and inquisitive, he is prevented from automati-cally participating in participants' schemas and modes, freeing him up to provide limited reparenting.

Group settings allow participants to play supportive or corrective roles for each other while sharing their experiences. A related pitfall is when group members are overly parentified and come to the aid of other members due to particular schemas and modes. It is the trainer's job to check such reactions in participants, and to explain to them the value of not succumbing to action-oriented behavior. Group members provide sufficient support to others simply by paying attention and listening without responding in an action-oriented way. It's important for these participants to learn how to deal with recognizing painful emotions in others. They do this by concentrating on their own experi-ence. When a member appears to be experiencing painful thoughts and emotions and the group responds by offering all sorts of tips and advice, the trainer can take the opportunity to start a mindful discus-sion on what sort of benefits these responses actually provide. The troubled individual in question will usually explain that, in spite of everyone's best intentions, their suggestions do little good. This person has either heard it all before and tried to no avail, or simply doesn't see how any of it could help. This is a reality check for the group, which can be used to illustrate the difference between being attention-oriented and action- or solution-oriented.

It is not uncommon for trainers to receive phone calls from participants outside of training hours. In some cases, as demonstrated below, the individual may be in crisis.

Andrea's primary schemas are Enmeshment/Undeveloped Self, Self-Sacrifice, Approval Seeking, and Vulnerability to Harm and Illness. She is on medication for her depression and anxiety symptoms. More often than not, she calls her trainer at the first sign of impending panic. Her typical story is that her medications aren't working, and that the mindfulness exercises aren't having any effect (switching to Vulnerable Child mode).

During one of Andrea's crisis calls, her trainer relates the following allegory: "Your experience reminds me of someone who never dared to go ice skating. One sunny day, this woman decided to confront her fears, and went skating on a pond near her house. The first 15 minutes were a bit bumpy, but as she went on, skating got easier and easier. So easy, in fact, that she stopped paying attention to where she was skating, and ended up falling through a hole in the ice. Totally submerged, she panicked and immediately tried to swim toward a bright spot up above. Expecting to breach the surface, she hit her head against the ice. Desperate, she tried to swim away, but everywhere she tried, there was only ice. Just when she decided there was no point in fighting, that she might as well give up, she had an insight: when you're stuck under the ice, look for a dark spot, because that's where you'll find a hole. Even though it felt totally counterintuitive, the woman decided to swim toward a dark spot in the ice. And just as she had hoped, there was indeed a hole."

For a moment, Andrea keeps silent, and then she laughs. She says: "I believe you're trying to tell me that I should actually pay attention to my feelings of panic, and surrender to them. That the very thing I fear is what I need to be mindful of."

It is important for trainers or other colleagues to be available for phone calls outside of training hours. The emotions experienced by participants in Vulnerable Child mode can be extremely intense. Another scenario involves group members in Punitive Parent mode, who may become angry with themselves and attempt self-injury. Another issue worth mentioning concerns the Detached Protector mode. Participants in this mode may detach and become highly indifferent toward themselves. This is an additional mode that can bring about self-mutilating acts or other destructive behavior. Let participants know that they should learn to recognize those moments, and call the available contacts for help. When trainers pick up a crisis call, they will do well to remain mindful and avoid action-oriented responses. In Andrea's case, an action-oriented state was clearly not required. Participants need to feel that they are being heard, that they have the trainer's full attention. Oftentimes, that is all it takes for people to see a way forward once more.

8

Conclusion

The Training Mindfulness and Schema Therapy is a detailed program intended to help bring awareness to the functioning of schemas and modes, learning to recognize the processes that shape our automatic responses. The automatic pilot switches on as soon as our schemas are triggered and we enter a certain mode.

Some people with personality problems will get all they need from just this training. They will internalize the principles of mindfulness and give it a permanent place in their lives, whether they hang on to the exercises learned in this training or find their own way.

Others may have only just begun their therapeutic process. They have started to become aware of their automatic pilot, and will continue their development through follow-up treatments or ongoing therapy. These individuals may benefit from regular refreshers of the material imparted in this training. A useful approach in therapy is to initiate and conclude every session with a brief mindfulness exercise. Therapists and patients alike will profit from continued emphasis on a therapeutic alliance where mindfulness and an open, inquisitive

Mindfulness and Schema Therapy: A Practical Guide, First Edition.
Michiel van Vreeswijk, Jenny Broersen and Ger Schurink.
© 2014 John Wiley & Sons, Ltd. Published 2014 by John Wiley & Sons, Ltd.

attitude are the norm. The mindfulness-based approach is highly compatible with the principle of limited parenting, so much so that it is described in Schema Therapy literature as a powerful therapeutic medium. Nonetheless, mindfulness remains one of the most challenging skills to be applied in daily life. This simple technique for focused awareness, free from automatic pilot, has been described by some as the equivalent to a professional sport. It requires constant practice from both the patient and therapist.

APPENDIX II-A

Test Result Example

Summary of Assessment Test Results

Mindfulness and Schema Therapy

Name: _____

Date of birth: _____

Date of assessment: _____

Assessed by: _____

Test material:

☐ BSI

☐ Schema questionnaire

☐ Modes questionnaire

☐ (Optional: additional personality questionnaire)

Test results:

Participant's BSI score relative to normal clinical values: _____

Participant's primary complaint _____

(Three highest-scoring BSI subscales)

1. _____

2. _____

3. _____

The participant rates *low/below average/average/high* on the schema questionnaire.

Mindfulness and Schema Therapy: A Practical Guide, First Edition.
Michiel van Vreeswijk, Jenny Broersen and Ger Schurink.
© 2014 John Wiley & Sons, Ltd. Published 2014 by John Wiley & Sons, Ltd.

Participant's three highest-scoring schemas are:

(Descriptions of participant's top three schemas + explanations based on schema information in the "Mindfulness and Schema Therapy" folder)

1. _____

2. _____

3. _____

The participant rates *low/below average/average/high* on the modes questionnaire.

Participant's three highest-scoring modes are:

(Descriptions of participant's top three modes + explanations based on mode information in the "Mindfulness and Schema Therapy" folder)

1. _____

2. _____

3. _____

In terms of personality, the participant is someone who:

(Results from the optional personality questionnaire, if included)

_____

_____

_____

_____

Therapist signature: _____

APPENDIX II-B

Mindfulness and Schema Therapy Handout

Bill has had several jobs. He is known as a hard worker and a perfectionist. He often works overtime (Unrelenting Standards/Hypocritical schema). Nevertheless, Bill frequently experiences conflict in the workplace. He believes his superiors don't show him enough appreciation, and that they fail to support him when he's under pressure (Emotional Deprivation schema). He is also critical of his coworkers, and thinks they should work more efficiently. Bill often feels lonely at work. At times he also feels misunderstood, unappreciated, and unsupported (Vulnerable Child mode). In this mode, he tends to work even harder and becomes more irritable while interacting with others.

Introduction

Schemas are deep-seated, long-established ways of thinking about yourself, others, and the world around you. These engrained and trusted perspectives influence what you perceive, how you behave, and what you feel. For example, people with the Unrelenting Standards/Hypocritical schema have a fixed perception that they need to do better, and that others should live up to their high standards and values too. These people are rarely satisfied with themselves or with other people, which leads to further irritation.

Mindfulness and Schema Therapy: A Practical Guide, First Edition.
Michiel van Vreeswijk, Jenny Broersen and Ger Schurink.
© 2014 John Wiley & Sons, Ltd. Published 2014 by John Wiley & Sons, Ltd.

When one or more schemas are triggered a particular mood (or mode) sets in. Each mode is characterized by specific behaviors and intense emotions. For instance, when the Unrelenting Standards/ Hypocritical schema and the Emotional Deprivation schema are activated, you might go into Vulnerable Child mode. This may happen when, in spite of your best efforts, someone leaves you high and dry— even when you would have been there for that person if they were in your situation. You feel lonely, misunderstood, and unsupported.

In Schema Therapy there are 19 schemas and 20 modes (described later in this section). It is assumed that everyone has schemas and modes, but that these are present to different degrees in different people. Furthermore, some people have a hard time dealing with their modes.

Alisha does not easily trust other people. She prefers to wait and see which way the wind blows. Even when some trust develops, she expects her trust to be abused eventually (Mistrust and/or Abuse schema). Alisha has a tendency to (unconsciously) seek out situations that can confirm her Mistrust and/or Abuse schema. She also tends to test people, and will eventually find something to convince her that she is being taken advantage of. During the mindfulness training, Alisha learns to be more conscious of her testing behavior, which she finds out is intimately tied to her Mistrust and/or Abuse schema. She starts to realize that everyone messes up from time to time, and people don't mess up just to hurt her. Alisha becomes aware of her tendency to categorize people as either good or bad, and that this is a detriment to herself as well as to others.

Mindfulness and Schema Therapy

One way in which we organize information is by dividing facts into right and wrong. It's a strategy with undeniable advantages. But schemas and modes influence this process in subtle and automatic ways, without us being aware of it. It is that unawareness—our inability to perceive more than we are used to perceiving—that can get us into trouble. Many problems arise or persist because we react to situations on automatic pilot, as if we are suffering from tunnel vision. This training program is designed to help you become more aware of your automatic pilot and the influence of your schemas and modes. You will learn how to disengage the automatic pilot. You will learn to observe your attitude, the situation, and your thoughts, feelings, and behavior with an open and curious mind. You will learn that thoughts, feelings, and behaviors come and go with equal ease. Being aware of what is, and letting it be, is what mindfulness is all about.

The training program consists of eight weekly meetings of an hour and a half each, in which you will practice mindfulness exercises together with a group. As homework you will be asked to practice these exercises four times a week. You will also carry out shorter mindfulness exercises on a daily basis. You will discuss your practice experiences with other members of the group. Reflecting on these exercises will help you become more aware of the way your schemas and modes operate. Together you will learn to experience what is, doing so without judgment or the need to react. The first step in developing mindfulness is learning how to avoid launching into doing-mode on automatic pilot.

In the second session of the mindfulness training, Jennifer expresses disappointment over the lack of visible results. She had expected to feel less emotional, ruminate less, and get more in touch with her body. Even though she has done the exercises every day, Jennifer has actually become more emotional and less in touch with her body. Another participant says she finds the exercises boring; that it's all too airy-fairy for her. Other participants say they enjoyed the exercises.

The therapist invites the group to mindfully and inquisitively attend to their reactions to the exercises. Are they harboring expectations for themselves, or for the exercises? What are they thinking? What kind of emotions do they feel? What sort of bodily sensations come up? The participants then discuss how easy it is for people to immediately jump into action-mode; how they tend to expect immediate results; and how difficult it is to just watch and see what happens, without wanting to do something about it right away.

Pitfalls

Schemas and modes often push people to immediately launch into action. As if something needs to be done right away. Mindfulness training will allow you to let go of that urge to act and to simply be aware. Taking time to step out of automatic pilot mode will improve the odds of recognizing your schemas and modes; of becoming more aware. Once you have gained that perspective you can mindfully consider which actions are appropriate to your situation. How you choose to behave will then be a conscious decision, rather than an automatic reaction.

This training can be difficult for people who are used to pushing away unpleasant feelings on a daily basis. Mindfulness exercises involve paying close attention to your feelings, so you may experience some serious discomfort. Experience shows, however, that emotions are most effectively dealt with when they are faced, not avoided. Doing so will allow you to take better care of yourself. On the other hand, continuing to avoid or ignore your emotions tends to seriously worsen your symptoms.

Another common pitfall happens when participants expect immediate results from the training. People wish to suffer less from their worries, sadness, anxiety, and pain. They become frustrated when the Mindfulness Training for Personality Problems program does not (directly) yield the results they desire. Their frustration can be difficult to accept. Participants should recognize that this training is not meant to wipe away their problems. The goal of the training is to develop a more mindful lifestyle; to become more aware of your

Conclusion

needs, feelings, thoughts, behaviors, bodily experience, and the influence of your schemas and modes. Our objective is not change per se, but improved awareness.

Definitions of the 19 Schemas and 20 Modes

Note: These schema and mode definitions have been taken from the *Wiley-Blackwell Handbook of Schema Therapy – Theory, Practice, and Research* (Van Vreeswijk, Broersen, & Nadort, 2012).

The 19 schemas

Emotional Deprivation
The individual expects that others will never or not adequately meet his primary emotional needs (e.g. for support, nurturance, empathy, and protection). He feels isolated and lonely.

Abandonment/Instability
The individual expects that significant others will eventually abandon him. Others are unreliable and unpredictable in their support and connection. When the individual feels abandoned he switches between feelings of anxiety, grief, and anger.

Mistrust and/or Abuse
The individual is convinced that others will intentionally abuse him in some way or that they will cheat or humiliate him. These feelings vary greatly and the individual is continuously on edge.

Social Isolation/Alienation
The individual feels isolated from the world and believes that he is not part of any community.

Defectiveness/Shame
The individual believes that he is internally flawed and bad. If others get close, they will realize this and withdraw from the

91

relationship. The feeling of being worthless often leads to a strong sense of shame.

Social Undesirability
The individual believes that he is socially inept and physically unattractive. He sees himself as boring, dull, and ugly.

Failure
The individual believes that he is incapable of performing as well as his peer group. He feels stupid and untalented.

Dependence/Incompetence
The individual feels extremely helpless and incapable of functioning independently. He is incapable of making day-to-day decisions and is often tense and anxious.

Vulnerability to Harm and Illness
The individual believes that imminent catastrophe will strike him and significant others, and that he is unable to prevent this.

Enmeshment/Undeveloped Self
The individual has an excessive emotional involvement and closeness with one or more significant others (often his parents), as a result of which he cannot develop his own identity.

Subjugation
The individual submits to the control of others in order to avoid negative consequences. The individual ignores his own needs because he fears conflict and punishment.

Self-Sacrifice
The individual focuses on voluntarily meeting the needs of others, whom he considers weaker than himself. If he pays attention to his

own needs, he feels guilty, and he gives priority to the needs of others. Finally, he becomes annoyed with the people he is looking after.

Approval Seeking*
The individual focuses excessively on gaining recognition, approval, and attention, at the expense of his own development and needs.

Emotional Inhibition
The individual inhibits emotions and impulses because he believes that any expression of feelings will harm others or lead to embarrassment, retaliation, or abandonment. He lacks spontaneity and stresses rationality.

Unrelenting Standards/Hypocritical
The individual believes that whatever he does is not good enough and that he must always strive harder. He is hypercritical of himself and others, and he is a perfectionist, rigid and extremely efficient. This is at the expense of pleasure, relaxation, and social contacts.

Negativity and Pessimism*
The individual is always focused on the negative aspects of life and ignores or plays down the positive aspects. He is frequently anxious and hyper-alert.

Punitiveness*
The individual believes that people should be harshly punished for making mistakes. He is aggressive, intolerant, impatient, and unforgiving.

Entitlement/Grandiosity
The individual believes that he is superior to others and entitled to special rights. He insists that he should be able to do or have what he wants, regardless of what others think. The core theme is power and being in control of situations or people.

Insufficient Self-Control/Self-Discipline
The individual has no tolerance of frustration and is unable to control his feelings and impulses. He cannot bear dissatisfaction or discomfort (pain, conflicts, or overexertion).

* These schemas are not yet identifiable using the Schema Questionnaire (YSQ).

The 20 modes

Vulnerable Child
The individual believes that nobody will fulfill his needs and that everyone will eventually abandon him. He mistrusts others and believes that they will abuse him. He feels worthless and expects rejection. He is ashamed of himself and he often feels excluded. He behaves like a small, vulnerable child who clings to the therapist for help, because he feels lonely and believes there is danger everywhere.

Angry Child
The individual feels intensely angry, enraged, and impatient because his core needs are not being met. He can also feel abandoned, humiliated, or betrayed. He expresses his anger in extreme manifestations, both verbal and nonverbal, just like a small child who has an outburst of anger.

Enraged Child
The individual feels enraged for the same reason as the Angry Child, but loses control. This is expressed in offensive and injurious actions toward people and objects, in the same way a small child hurts his parents.

Impulsive Child
The individual wants to satisfy his (non-core) desires in a selfish and uncontrolled manner. He cannot control his feelings and impulses and he becomes enraged and infuriated when his (non-core) desires or impulses are not met. He often behaves like a spoiled child.

94

Undisciplined Child
The individual has no tolerance of frustration and cannot force himself to finish routine or boring tasks. He cannot bear dissatisfaction or discomfort (pain, conflict, or overexertion) and he behaves like a spoiled child.

Happy Child
The individual feels loved, satisfied, protected, understood, and validated. He is self-confident and feels competent, appropriately autonomous, and in control. He can react spontaneously, is adventurous and optimistic, and plays like a happy, young child.

Compliant Surrender
The individual devotes himself to the desire of others in order to avoid negative consequences. He suppresses his own needs or emotions and bottles up his aggression. He behaves subserviently and passively, and hopes to gain approval by being obedient. He tolerates abuse from other people.

Detached Protector
The individual cuts off strong feelings because he believes that such feelings are dangerous and can get out of hand. He withdraws from social contacts and tries to cut off his feelings (sometimes this leads to dissociation). The individual feels empty, bored, and depersonalized. He may adopt a cynical or pessimistic attitude to keep others at arm's length.

Detached Self-Soother
The individual seeks distraction in order not to feel negative emotions. He achieves this by self-soothing behavior (e.g. sleeping or substance abuse) or by self-stimulating activities (being fanatical or occupied with work, the Internet, sport, or sex).

Self-Aggrandizer
The individual believes that he is superior to others and entitled to special rights. He insists that he should be able to do or have what he

wants, regardless of what others think. He shows off and denigrates others to augment his self-esteem.

Bully and Attack

The individual wants to prevent being controlled or hurt by others, and therefore he tries to be in control of them. He uses threats, intimidation, aggression, and force to this end. He always wants to be in a dominant position, and takes sadistic pleasure in hurting others.

Punitive Parent

The individual is aggressive, intolerant, impatient, and unforgiving toward himself. He is always self-critical and feels guilty. He is ashamed of his mistakes and believes he has to be punished severely for them. This mode is a reflection of what (one of) the parents or other educators used to say to the individual in order to belittle or punish him.

Demanding Parent

The individual feels that he must fulfill rigid rules, norms, and values. He must be extremely efficient in meeting these. He believes that whatever he does is never good enough and that he must strive harder. Therefore, he pursues his highest standard until it is perfect, at the expense of rest and pleasure. He is also never satisfied with the result. These rules and norms are also internalized by (one of) the parents.

Healthy Adult

The individual has positive and neutralized thoughts and feelings about himself. He does things that are good for him and this leads to healthy relationships and activities. The Healthy Adult mode isn't maladaptive.

Angry Protector**

The individual uses a wall of anger to protect himself against others, considered to be a threat. He keeps others at a safe distance with great displays of rage. However, his anger is more under control than that in the Angry or Enraged Child.

*Obsessive Over-Controller***
The individual tries to protect himself against supposed or actual threats by keeping everything under extreme control. He uses repetitions or rituals to achieve this.

*Paranoid***
The individual tries to protect himself against supposed or actual threats by containing others and exposing their real intentions.

*Conning and Manipulative***
The individual cheats, lies, or manipulates in order to achieve a specific aim, the purpose of which is to victimize others or to avoid punishment.

*Predator***
The individual eliminates threats, rivals, obstacles, or enemies in a cold, ruthless, calculating way.

*Attention-Seeker***
The individual tries to obtain the approval and attention of others by exaggerated behavior, erotomania, or grandiosity.

** These modes have not (yet) been added to the Schema Mode Inventory (SMI-1).

APPENDIX II-C

Schema and Modes Worksheet

Name:................................

Schema 1:..........................   Mode 1:..........................

Schema 2:..........................   Mode 2:..........................

Schema 3:..........................   Mode 3:..........................

The sheets are used to rate schema mindfulness scores on a weekly basis, graded on a scale from 0 to 10 (0 = schema not at all mindfully observed, 10 = schema observed with full mindfulness).

	Score Week 1	Score Week 2	Score Week 3	Score Week 4	Score Week 5	Score Week 6	Score Week 7	Score Week 8
Schema 1								
Schema 2								
Schema 3								

Mindfulness and Schema Therapy: A Practical Guide, First Edition.
Michiel van Vreeswijk, Jenny Broersen and Ger Schurink.
© 2014 John Wiley & Sons, Ltd. Published 2014 by John Wiley & Sons, Ltd.

Part III
Participant Workbook

9

Participant Workbook

This workbook has been developed specifically for the training Mindfulness and Schema Therapy. It provides structure and information about the sessions, and functions as an aid to help retain the knowledge acquired during training. At the following website, http://www.mfvanvreeswijk.com, patients can buy mindfulness exercises (audio files), like the ones in this book. We consider these required listening, as experience has shown the training to be more effective when participants practice on their own, outside of the group meetings.

The workbook is divided into eight sessions and two follow-up sessions. It includes explanations of the core concepts, including mindfulness, schemas, and modes, and discusses some of the questions pertinent to each session. Each of the exercises is described in detail. Some participants benefit from rereading the exercises after carrying them out. Homework for subsequent sessions is listed at the end of every session.

Mindfulness and Schema Therapy: A Practical Guide, First Edition.
Michiel van Vreeswijk, Jenny Broersen and Ger Schurink.
© 2014 John Wiley & Sons, Ltd. Published 2014 by John Wiley & Sons, Ltd.

Session 1: Schemas, Modes, and Mindfulness Training

Schemas, schema modes, and schema coping

Schemas are deeply rooted, firmly anchored ways of perceiving ourselves, others, and the world around us. These ways of perceiving are shaped by life experiences. Schemas can be quite useful because they simplify our realities; they make the enormous amount of information we face on a daily basis more manageable. Schemas become a problem, however, when they turn into fixed patterns of thinking and perceiving, thus depriving us of the ability to make conscious decisions across various situations. Eventually we can lose the flexibility required for living our lives in healthy, appropriate ways.

Schemas are often triggered by specific situations or interactions with people, and may cause strong, painful emotions to arise. When one or more schemas are activated at the same time or in rapid succession, it is common to end up in a counterproductive mood or moods (i.e. modes). In such modes, our behavior is typically less healthy than it would be under different circumstances, or if another person was in the same situation.

Frank has a hard time opening up and making himself vulnerable to others. When he goes to parties, he often feels as if he doesn't belong; as if other people find him strange or uninteresting. When a friend of his sees him at a party one night, she comments on how quiet Frank is and says that she would like to see him opening up and sharing once in a while. Frank totally closes up. He finds himself withdrawing from his friend, his mind blank and at a loss for words. She tells him they are drifting apart, that she regrets this because she enjoys his company and would like to get to know him better. Frank is sad to hear this, but instead of sharing his feelings, he crawls further into his shell and orders another beer. He drinks eight of them that night, hoping the alcohol will help him relax and speak more freely.

Nineteen schemas and twenty modes have been identified in the general population thus far. They are listed in Table 9.1. For a more detailed description of each schema and mode, please refer to Appendix II-B.

Table 9.1 Schemas and modes

Nineteen schemas	Twenty modes
Emotional Deprivation	Vulnerable Child
Abandonment/Instability	Angry Child
Mistrust and/or Abuse	Enraged Child
Social Isolation/Alienation	Impulsive Child
Defectiveness/Shame	Undisciplined Child
Social Undesirability	Happy Child
Failure	Compliant Surrender
Dependence/Incompetence	Detached Protector
Vulnerability to Harm and Illness	Detached Self-Soother
Enmeshment/Undeveloped Self	Self-Aggrandizer
Subjugation	Bully and Attack
Self-Sacrifice	Punitive Parent
Approval Seeking*	Demanding Parent
Emotional Inhibition	Healthy Adult
Unrelenting Standards/Hypocritical	Angry Protector**
Negativity and Pessimism*	Obsessive Over-Controller**
Punitiveness*	Paranoid**
Entitlement/Grandiosity	Conning and Manipulative**
Insufficient Self-Control/Self-Discipline	Predator**
	Attention-seeker**

*These schemas are not yet identifiable using the Schema Questionnaire (YSQ).
**These modes have not (yet) been added to the Schema Mode Inventory (SMI-1).
Source: van Vreeswijk, Broersen, & Nadort, 2012. Reproduced with permission of Wiley.

Frank's example illustrates how Social Isolation/Alienation, Emotional Inhibition, and Defectiveness/Shame schemas can be manifested in the Vulnerable Child mode, after which Detached Protector and Detached Self-Soother coping modes are engaged. Frank maintains his schemas through the use of alcohol, which appears to make him more eloquent. This represents a schema avoidance strategy; one which enables him to conclude that his schemas are justified, and that he needs alcohol to interact with people.

In the example above, Frank demonstrates one of three schema-coping styles (ways of handling difficult/painful situations) by which schemas are upheld. There are three main strategies that allow schemas to survive: schema avoidance, schema overcompensation, and schema surrender.

Schema avoidance is behavior meant to escape from or prevent situations that can trigger schemas or bring them up in conversation. Examples of potential schema avoidance strategies include substance abuse, excessive computer use, hard work, sleep, daydreaming, and watching TV.

Schema overcompensation is much like shouting over the top of your schemas. In this form of behavior we deny vulnerability and ignore our sensitive areas. We do precisely what we find difficult, unpleasant, or frightening in an over-the-top way in order to prove our schemas wrong.

Schema surrender involves seeking out information that confirms a schema. Any facts that contradict our schemas are basically glossed over or ignored. We only notice those aspects of a situation that support our schemas.

The following example describes schema overcompensating and schema surrendering behavior in a woman with Insufficient Self-Control/Self-Discipline and Emotional Deprivation as her main schemas. Her predominant modes are the Vulnerable Child and Demanding Parent.

Irene is lonely. Her best friend has cancelled their shopping date and her husband will be home late due to a meeting at work. She grows unhappier by the minute, until she spontaneously decides to go downtown on her own. She thinks she can have fun by herself and she's going to prove it. Strolling down the busy shopping street, Irene seems to feel much happier. Passing an expensive store, she notices something she has had her eye on for a while. She doesn't believe she really deserves this expensive item, but then again … Irene decides to call her husband to tell him about her day and to ask if it's okay to buy this item. But when he answers the phone he's in the middle of a meeting. He says he doesn't have time for her now and asks if they can talk about it tomorrow. Irene hangs up feeling disappointed and lonely. It's just as she thought: no one ever has time for her. Whenever she needs someone, no one is there to listen, even though she's always there for other people.

Training mindfulness and schema therapy

We are not truly aware of most of the things we do. When riding a bicycle, for example, we're not constantly thinking about moving the left pedal with our left foot, and the right pedal with our right foot. Obviously this automatic pilot has its advantages: it permits us to do several things at once. But there are also disadvantages. We might cycle right past our destination if we are too busy thinking about something else.

Similar oversights can happen with schemas and modes. Ideally their purpose is to make our world easier to understand, and to guide our actions under different circumstances. But schemas and modes can become problematic when they run automatically and persistently. We end up losing sight of the fact that our schemas and modes are shaping our behavior. They deprive us of the ability to consciously decide how to act.

In the following eight weeks you will learn to recognize when your schemas and modes have been triggered. By becoming more aware of what happens when a schema is activated, you will develop greater mindfulness of yourself, others, and your environment. You will bring greater awareness to the unpleasant thoughts and feelings that accompany your schemas, instead of denying, avoiding, or giving in to them. The experience of your body will become a point of focus, and you will learn to perceive physical sensations with mindfulness and acceptance, rather than fear, sadness, or anger. Breathing will become an ever-present anchor to rely on when your schemas and modes are (strongly) triggered, helping you to recognize when you are in the grips of a mental event, which is distorting your view of reality. Developing the ability to watch schema-triggering moments from a mindful distance will allow you to react to situations in life with greater awareness.

This training is not intended to make your painful emotions, thoughts, and actions go away—though of course this would be a wonderful bonus. Rather than try to correct or escape your inner experiences, your goal will be to allow them and observe them. This approach will create more room for conscious decision making, letting you react to situations independently of your emotions, schemas, and modes.

Example: Automatic schema- and mode-based reaction

> ### Automatic reaction

John is at a party and sees everyone around him talking and laughing.
(Trigger)

$$\downarrow \qquad\qquad \downarrow$$

John feels as if he doesn't belong. That he is different or inferior.

(Schema triggered; Social Isolation/Alienation and Defectiveness/ Shame)

John feels himself getting restless, unhappy, and wishes not to feel anything. His mind becomes empty and muddled. He couldn't care less about what others think of him.
(Mode triggered; Detached Protector)

John withdraws further and finds a seat in the corner of the room, drinking one beer after another. When someone approaches and asks him to dance, he bluntly declines. He watches everyone else having fun, but fails to notice the other people standing against the wall on the side.
(Schema coping, avoidance, and surrender)

Example: Mindfulness-based reaction

Mindful reaction

John is at a party and sees everyone around him talking and laughing.
(Trigger)

John feels as if he doesn't belong. That he is different or inferior.
(Schema triggered; Social Isolation/Alienation and Defectiveness/ Shame)

John feels himself getting restless, unhappy, and wishes not to feel anything. His mind becomes empty and muddled. He couldn't care less about what others think of him. Part of him feels lonely, wants to leave, wants not to feel. This healthy part of John knows it is important not to fall into automatic pilot mode. He knows it is important to be mindful of his feelings and needs, but also to remain aware of his surroundings. (Mode triggered; Detached Protector and Healthy Adult)

John focuses on breathing. Every time he trails off and gets dragged down by his schemas, he recognizes the influence of his schemas and modes on his point of view. By continuing to mindfully observe himself and his surroundings, John notices his feelings of sadness and loneliness changing. He realizes there are other people standing against the wall, away from the frenzy of the party. John decides to join them and starts a conversation.
(Mindfulness-based approach to dealing with schema and mode activation).

Practice, Practice, Practice

Regular practice, both during and after training, is essential. Learning to respond mindfully to schemas and modes takes a lot of time and practice. You can't expect something that has become engrained over years and years to simply disappear overnight. This process will contain moments of frustration or encounters with (painful) emotions you would rather avoid. These are normal reactions. The goal is to become aware of these moments, to recognize your schemas, and to understand that they will do anything to stay in control. Gradually you will develop the ability to decide between a life directed by schemas and modes, or a life directed by your own free will.

This book contains various exercises, some of which will prove more suitable for you than others. Try each of them more than once. Only after you have gone through all the exercises can you consciously determine which ones work best for you.

Exercise 1.1   The Raisin Exercise[1]

We will start the course with an experience-based exercise. I am going to give you an object. Take this object in the palm of your hand. Inspect it as if you've never seen anything like it before. Pretend you have come from Mars and have just arrived on Earth; this is the first thing you see, and you have no idea what it is.

- Study the object closely.
  (20 second pause)
- Examine it with great curiosity, as if you've never seen anything like it in your entire life.
  (20 second pause)
- Roll it around between your thumb and index finger. Explore the outer ridges catching the light, and the darker areas inside the folds.
  (20 second pause).
- Let your eyes move all over this object, as if for the very first time.
  (20 second pause).
- Feel the surface and sense its substance, its elasticity, its weight.
  (20 second pause).
- And while you're doing this, if you experience any thoughts like: "This is a really weird exercise," or
  "What's the point of this," or "This is not doing anything for me," then try to see those thoughts as mere ideas—nothing more than that—and turn your attention back to the object.
  (20 second pause).
- Bring the object up to your ear. Squeeze it and roll it between your fingers. Listen carefully.
  (20 second pause).

[1]   This exercise is not included on the website.

- Now determine whether the object has an odor. Hold it to your nose and smell it. Also notice the motion of your arm and hand while doing this.
- Then take another look at it.
  (20 second pause).
- You are about to put the object in your mouth. Slowly bring it up to your lips, noticing that your hand and arm know exactly how to perform this movement. Perhaps you'll even become aware of the saliva entering your mouth, starting from the moment you decide to place the object in it.
  (20 second pause).
- Once the object has been carefully placed in your mouth—don't bite into it just yet—be aware of how that feels.
- When ready, gently bite into the object and notice the flavors that emerge.
  (20 second pause).
- Slowly start to chew. Notice more of the saliva entering your mouth, notice how the texture of the object changes as you chew, notice all the little sounds that chewing and swallowing make. Be aware of the different flavors that appear.
  (20 second pause).
- Finally, pay close attention to the sensation of swallowing the object. Feel it moving down your throat and esophagus, and toward your stomach.
  (20 second pause).
- Realize that your body has just become heavier, by exactly the weight of this object!

Body Scan exercise instructions

The Body Scan exercise is meant to increase your awareness of the sensations in your body, and to improve your ability to maintain that awareness. You will focus your attention on physical experiences as they arise; without reacting, wanting to change them, or accepting/rejecting them.

The Body Scan is not intended to make you relax or calm down. That may be a side effect but it is not the goal.

Say, for instance, you feel pain somewhere in your body. Direct your attention to that feeling. If the pain becomes stronger or weaker, become aware of that change. The goal is to become mindful of physical sensations and of how they change. Whatever you are sensing in a given moment, try not to change the experience in any way!

You will notice that whenever you try to focus on something, distractions eventually arise. This is to be expected, as is the nature of the mind. Our advice during these exercises is not to worry about distractions, and not to interpret them as failures. If you notice your thoughts trailing off, this means that you have actually succeeded in stepping out of automatic pilot mode—which is precisely the point! Simply pause, take notice, and come back to your original point of focus. And make sure to do so in a kind and gentle way. This exercise will run more smoothly if you gently bring your mind back to your breath each time you notice it has wandered, rather than judging yourself, which tends to lead to further distracting thoughts. With practice, your ability to recognize distracting thoughts will improve.

Emotions may also sidetrack your attention. You can bring yourself back on track through mindfulness of the body. This will ground your awareness in the physical component of your emotions, rather than the spiral of emotionally laden thoughts.

During the Body Scan, each moment and each part of your body entering awareness will present you with new experiences to be observed. Hold your attention over each successive area for the duration of a few breaths. You can use the rhythm of your breath for support, moving to a new area during the inhalation. We will prompt you with the words, "Breathe into the area ... and out of it." If at this point of the exercise your mind has already trailed off, then be mindful of what distracted you, as that is your actual experience at the time. Once you have reflected on the distraction, calmly return to the exercise. Even if you are sidetracked one thousand times, come back to the exercise—gently—another thousand times...

If you find listening to the audio file helpful for this exercise, you may use it for a while, but eventually you should be able to perform the body scan on your own. Practicing at your own pace will allow you to be more thorough and to spend extra time on areas experiencing more sensations. During the training the exercise is done while seated, but at home you may try it lying down. The important thing is to practice the body scan every day, and to do so without any expectations. Just turn it into a daily activity. Start afresh with each new exercise. Be curious about what sort of experiences your body presents, and how much detail about the bodily sensations you become aware of. The more mindful you become, the more you will notice connections between what happens in your body and what goes on in your mind. Moreover, as you become more adept at noticing physical sensations, so will it grow easier to respond to and take care of your body.

Exercise 1.2   Body Scan

This exercise can be carried out in a seated or reclined position— as long as you are somewhere you won't be disturbed. While meditating, keep your back straight and relaxed, with your head gently balanced between your shoulders, and your feet side by side on the floor.

You may wish to close your eyes, or keep them half open. Find out what works best for maintaining your focus.

- Begin the exercise by directing your attention toward the sensation of breathing. Take some time to experience the movement of your belly as it follows the rhythm of your breath in a consistent, natural way, without trying to change it… (2 minutes)
- After focusing on the rhythmic motion of your belly and your breath, become mindful of the area at the top of your head. Breathe into and out of this area a number of times.

Find out which sensations you can become aware of on the top of your head.

- Now move your attention to your forehead. Take a number of breaths into and out of this area. Notice whether your breathing stays in the foreground or the background during this part of the exercise. Watch for any physical sensations in your forehead.

- Now move to the area around your eyes. Spend a number of breaths focusing on this part of your face. See what kind of physical sensations are going on around your eyes. Do this as mindfully as possible, in a playful and relaxed manner... Breathe into and out of this area for some time.

- From here on in, I will only name the parts of your body for you to focus on and observe. Cheeks and jaw ... neck ... shoulders ... upper left arm ... lower left arm ... left hand ... and the fingers of your left hand ... upper right arm ... lower right arm ... right hand ... and the fingers on your right hand ... chest ... belly ... upper back ... lower back ... waist ... pelvic area ... upper left leg ... lower left leg ... left foot ... and the toes of your left foot ... upper right leg ... lower right leg ... right foot ... and the toes on your right foot.

- Finally, become mindful of your body as a whole. Take a few breaths which reach from the crown of your head, down to your feet, and back again ... (1 minute).

- Turn your attention to the breath once more. Be mindful of your stomach as it moves along with your breath in a consistent, natural way.

- Every new experience with the Body Scan exercise can be seen as a pristine opportunity to discover what kinds of physical sensations will arise.

- We will now complete the exercise. If you've kept your eyes closed, open them now. Become aware of the space you are in, and try moving around a bit or doing some light stretches ....

Homework

Many of the following handouts will be reused in several sessions. Please photocopy the forms.

- Homework assignment: Everyday Mindfulness (Appendix III-A), eight copies
- Homework sheet: Fill in Five-Facet M Questionnaire (Appendix III-B), four copies
- Homework sheet: Cultivating Schema Mindfulness (Appendix III-C), eight copies
- Homework sheet: Writing a Summary (Appendix III-D), eight copies
- Audio files exercises: Four times per week: Body Scan (1.2)
- Bring your notebook (with your schema mindfulness scores) to the following session
- Read the text for Session 1

Session 2: Mindfulness of Your Environment

Schemas and modes are often activated so quickly that we cannot recognize or understand what triggered them and how. Because of this we may feel as if something outside our control is pushing our buttons, leaving us with no control at all. However, a number of things happen before a schema is triggered, and we can become aware of them.

The Body Scan helps you become more mindful of the body's physical sensations and the schema triggering and reaction patterns that may follow. The Mindfulness of Your Environment exercise provides a way to broaden your mindfulness to include what is happening around you as well. It can amplify or alter your attention and point of view. But whether there are such changes or not, the main objective is simply to be mindful. Before practicing this exercise with the group, we will first discuss our experiences with the Body Scan and Everyday Mindfulness exercises. See the example below:

Dorothy has only practiced the Everyday Mindfulness exercise a few times over the past week. During the discussion it emerges that she did not set scheduled exercise times, but only practiced when she happened to remember. When she did do the exercise, Dorothy noticed that her thinking would easily get sidetracked into thoughts about her job and her to-do list for the day. She also noticed her tendency to brush her teeth very roughly. She initiated a few additional moments of mindfulness over the course of the week, for instance, while taking a walk or enjoying a cup of coffee.

The group discussion helps Dorothy become aware of how much time she spends worrying and how easily she gets distracted. She also recognizes her difficulty setting time apart for homework and other activities. Only after finishing all her work does she allow any time for herself (Unrelenting Standards/Hypocritical schema).

Exercises

Exercise 2.1   Mindfulness of Your Environment

As long as we live, we breathe. We spend most of our lives blissfully unaware of how fast we breathe, how deeply we breathe, and how our breath changes throughout the day. It is a natural process that takes place by itself, and the goal of this exercise is to become more aware of how that happens. You will do this without actually changing the way you breathe. The ability to focus on your breath will provide you with an anchor to rely on whenever you find yourself struggling with emotions, schemas, or modes.

Mindful breathing

- Sit down in a chair with an upright backrest. Keep your spine straight without leaning back.
- Allow your back to find a straight, comfortable, and dignified position.
- Rest your feet flat on the floor.
- Close your eyes or keep a softly focused gaze on a point in front of you.
- Become aware of the sensations of contact and pressure in the areas of your body touching the floor and chair. Spend a few minutes examining these sensations, just as you did in the Body Scan.
- Become mindful of your breathing, paying attention to where in the body you feel your breath. You can focus on the sensations in your belly as you inhale and exhale, or on the feeling of air rushing in and out of your nose with every breath. Concentrate on whichever area most strongly experiences the breath.
- Whenever you find yourself trailing off, quietly compliment yourself on being so mindful. Remember: Everyone gets distracted, and catching yourself at it means you get a new opportunity to become mindful of your breath. Try to see every inhalation and exhalation as a totally new event deserving all of your attention.
- Consider the moments between breathing in and out. What are those like? Sometimes there is a long pause in the breath, sometimes a short one. Where do you feel your breath? Does it change?
- Stay mindful of breathing and of the natural variations in that process. Train your attention on the beginning of each breath and hold it there until it expires, doing so for every breath. Notice when you get distracted and then come back to the breath.

Mindful listening

- After focusing on breathing for a while, begin to notice the sounds around you. Be mindful of any sounds that draw your attention, holding them in your awareness. Don't concern yourself with who or what is making these sounds. Simply notice how they come and go, when they are loud, and when they are soft.
- Pay attention to the differences between sounds; variations in texture and tone, distance and proximity; how sounds come closer or move away from you.

Mindfulness of physical sensations

- Expand your attention of the breath to the rest of your body. What is going on? Where do you feel any sensations? Does it tickle or itch? Is there tension? Pulsation? What happens when you focus on that feeling? Does it change? Become stronger or weaker? Does it disappear?
- Watch what happens when you deepen your awareness of the physical sensations in your body. Permit those feelings to exist without acting to change them. All bodily sensations follow a natural, innate processes.
- When you notice your bodily awareness fading, or if your attention has become sidetracked, go back to the physical anchor of your attention: the breath. From there you can expand your awareness to include the feelings in your body once more.

Mindfulness of thoughts

- If your mindful breathing gets distracted by thoughts or images in your mind, become aware of that distraction. Allow thoughts to come and go, without getting caught up in them and the stories they unavoidably weave in your mind. Be mindful of thoughts rising out of the depths of your mind and sinking back down. You may notice recurring thoughts representing familiar patterns and sequences. Reaching and maintaining a level of mindfulness of your thinking is the first step toward consciously choosing your reaction to thoughts. Being mindful helps you to avoid the trap of the automatic pilot.

- Notice what else happens to you as you give your thoughts free rein. There is no need to interfere; thoughts naturally follow the pattern of appearing and disappearing. They are only thoughts. If and when you realize you have become drawn into thinking, simply return to the breath.

Mindfulness of emotions

- Any emotions that enter awareness are permitted to exist. Give them your attention. What kind of emotions are they? How strong are they? Observe them without judging them as good or bad. Study them as though they are being experienced for the first time. Inspect them with curiosity, as you would if they were entirely unfamiliar to you. Now see if you can observe your emotions without getting sucked into the stories behind them. If you do get distracted by thoughts, or if you are uncomfortable facing your emotions like this, then come back to the breath. Once you are back in a mindful state, try to focus on your emotions again.

- We all tend to form a habit of labeling feelings as either pleasant or unpleasant. We learn to hold on to what feels good and run away from what is unpleasant or boring. This causes what are essentially neutral events to acquire an emotional value. Try to let your feelings exist without getting stuck in the thoughts and memories behind them.

- Study your body to determine where your emotions are being felt. What do your feelings look like? Imagine them as waves in an ocean, appearing and disappearing. Some waves are high and some are low, but every wave is destined to rise and fall.

Choiceless awareness

- If sounds, thoughts, images, or emotions appear in the background of your awareness, just let them be.
- Focus on your breath. If sounds, thoughts, images, or emotions enter the foreground of your awareness, then be mindful of whatever is there. Observe it consciously and continue to be mindful of whatever else presents itself.
- When you find yourself hesitating between the objects of your awareness, then focus on your breath. It is an anchor that is always there for you. We are now ready to bring this exercise to an end. Before moving forward with your day, consider bringing your experiences during this exercise with you into daily life. Did you arrive at any insights? Did you experience any moments of calm, silence, or harmony? If so, mindfully carry these over to the upcoming activities. Now I will slowly count to three; at three, you may open your eyes.
- Before switching back to doing-mode, spend a few moments being mindful of yourself and your present environment... 1... 2... 3.
- Spend around 20 minutes on this exercise each time you practice. Pay close attention to what you observe. Be mindful of every moment, every physical sensation, every thought, every emotion, and every sound. Whenever you have trouble focusing, you can rely on the breath to anchor you in mindfulness.

Homework

- Homework assignment: Everyday Mindfulness (Appendix III-A)
- Homework sheet: Cultivating Schema Mindfulness (Appendix III-C)
- Homework sheet: Writing a Summary (Appendix III-D)

- Audio files exercises: Body Scan (1.2) and Mindful of Your Environment (2.1)
- Read the text on Session 2

Session 3: Mindful Breathing

It is difficult to be mindful when we are worried or extremely busy. Busy activity puts the body in an action-oriented state, ready to fight or flee. Emotions like fear and anger can be amplified or not experienced at all. Our heart rate increases while our breathing speeds up and becomes shallow. Before we know it the mind is dragged down in a whirlpool of thoughts, causing us to lose a big chunk of external awareness. As a result we miss important (and not-so-important) signals in the environment—including evidence that contradict our schemas. We may overlook information that could have calmed us down, left us more at ease. In this chapter we pay close attention to the breath. Breathing serves as an exceptionally useful mindfulness aid.

Exercises

Exercise 3.1   Three Minute Breathing Space

We would like to start this brief exercise right away, so please assume the proper posture as soon as you are seated.

- Relax, sitting with your back straight but not stiff. Let a sense of presence and alertness fill your body. If you feel comfortable doing so, close your eyes. Your first step is to become aware, truly aware of what is happening in the here and now. Be mindful of your thoughts. What is going on inside your mind?

- See your thoughts as mental activity. We can simply observe, noting any emotions that arise. Pay special attention to any thoughts that are linked to unpleasant feelings. Rather than avoiding or pushing them away, acknowledge those feelings as they arise. You might say to yourself, about your feelings, "Ah, so you guys are here. This is what's happening right now." The same goes for any physical experiences.

- Do you notice any tension or other physical sensations? Again, be observant and simply register what you notice. "Okay, this is what's happening right now." You are being mindful of your inner world.

- You have exited automatic pilot mode. The next step is to focus your attention on one single thing: the experience of breathing.

- You can begin to concentrate on the rhythmic motion of the belly as it rises and falls with every breath.

- Spend about a minute on your belly. From moment to moment, breath after breath, so that each inhalation and each exhalation is consciously experienced.

- Center your awareness in the movement of your belly and, using the breath as your anchor, become fully present in the here and now.

- It is time for step three. When you are ready, let your attention expand to encompass your entire body.

- You are now mindful of the breath and of your body, with greater spatial awareness; an appreciation of the body as a whole.

- Stay mindful of the breath, as though your whole body is breathing.

- Holding all of it in a softer, more spatial awareness.

- Now I will slowly count to three; at three, you may open your eyes. Before switching back to doing-mode, just spend a few moments being mindful of yourself and your present environment ... 1... 2... 3.

Tip

Perform the Breathing Room exercise three times a day. It needn't take long; just a few minutes each day will stimulate the development of mindfulness. You may also find it helpful to combine these exercises with daily activities, like eating. Linking mindful breathing to something you do on a daily basis will help to make it a consistent part of your being.

Exercise 3.2   Mindfulness of Painful Memories

- Sit down in a chair with an upright backrest. Keep your spine straight without leaning back.
- Allow your back to find a straight, comfortable, and dignified position.
- Rest your feet flat on the floor.
- Close your eyes or keep a softly focused gaze on a point in front of you.
- Become aware of the sensation of contact and pressure in the areas of your body touching the floor and chair. Spend a few minutes examining these sensations, just as you did in the Body Scan.
- Become mindful of breathing, paying attention to where in the body you feel your breath. You can focus on the sensations in your belly as you inhale and exhale, or on the feeling of air rushing in and out of your nose with every breath. Concentrate on whichever area most strongly experiences the breath.
- Start to let specific memories, images, sounds, or smells appear in your mind; things that bother you, worry you, or

hurt you. They could be memories from your childhood, your teens, or from adulthood. Or perhaps an event in the future, something you aren't looking forward to. Feel the tension rising as you contemplate these memories or images. Be mindful as you allow them to unfold. Where are you now? How old are you? What do you see? Are other people present? What are they doing or saying? What kind of thoughts are going through your mind at this moment? What else can you feel? How strong are those feelings?

- Be mindful of your breath. Where in the body do you experience it? Focus on where the breath is most present. Be accepting of the emotions, thoughts, images, and physical sensations that appear. Some people find it helpful to speak tenderly to themselves, saying "This is my experience, and I accept it just the way it is. There is no need to change it. I can allow it to be."
- Spend a few more minutes being mindful of your breath. Whenever you find yourself trailing off, take notice of it with an easygoing, accepting attitude, and then return to the breath. Now I will slowly count to three, after which you may open your eyes. Before going back into doing-mode, take a few moments to become aware of your presence and the world around you... 1... 2... 3.

Exercise 3.3   Mindful Walking

- Find some place to go for a walk. It can be indoors or outside.
- Stand with your feet approximately 10–15 centimeters apart. Keep your knees slightly bent to allow for some bounce.
- Let your arms hang freely by your side, and look ahead with a softly focused gaze.

- Be mindful of the bottom of your feet and feel their contact with the floor. Sense how the weight of your body passes through your legs and feet to the ground. Slightly bend your knees a few times to emphasize the presence of your legs and feet.
- When you are ready, shift the weight of your body to your right leg. Notice the new sensation in your legs and feet, as your right leg now supports most of your weight, and your left leg feels lighter.
- Raise your left heel off the floor and feel the slight strain in your calf muscles.
- Slowly roll your left foot up until only your toes touch the floor. Be mindful of the changing sensations in your legs and feet.
- Now raise your left foot and carefully move it forwards.
- Be mindful of the feeling of your leg and foot gliding through the air, before you place your heel back on the floor in front of you.
- Let the rest of your foot come down as you gradually shift your weight to the left side of your body.
- Now sense how your left leg and foot get heavier as you prepare to take the next step with your right.
- Once you are supported by your left leg, raise your right foot off the floor and slowly move it forwards.
- Be mindful of the changing sensations in your legs and feet while moving forward.
- Be mindful of your right heel as it makes contact with the floor.
- Once your right foot is firmly planted on the floor, shift your weight to that side of the body.
- Stay aware of the continuously changing sensations in both legs and feet.
- Begin walking around.

- Be mindful of each step, giving unbroken attention to the feeling of your leg muscles moving and your soles touching the floor.
- If and when you turn around, try to appreciate of the complex sequence of movements your body makes while changing direction, and then continue walking.
- Keep moving back and forth, being as mindful as you can of the sensations in your legs and feet.
- Maintain your softly focused gaze as you look straight ahead.
- When you notice your attention drawing away from the experience of walking, go back to being mindful of your legs and feet.
- Just as you used your breath in seated meditation, use the contact between your feet and the floor as an anchor. This contact will ground you in the here and now.
- Continue walking in this way for 10 to 15 minutes, or longer if you wish.
- When you begin the walking exercise, start off slow so you can get used to being mindful. Once you get the hang of it, pick up to whatever speed is comfortable for you. However, if you feel rushed or restless when starting off, try launching into it at a rapid pace. Gradually reduce your speed as you begin to calm down.
- Try to practice this form of mindfulness as often as possible in your normal day-to-day walking.

Homework

- Homework assignment: Everyday Mindfulness (Appendix III-A)
- Homework sheet: Fill in Five-Facet M Questionnaire (Appendix III-B)
- Homework sheet: Cultivating Schema Mindfulness (Appendix III-C)

- Homework sheet: Writing a Summary (Appendix III-D)
- Audio files exercises: Body Scan (1.1), Breathing Room (3.1), Mindfulness of Painful Memories (3.2)
- Exercise: Mindful Walking (3.3)
- Read the text for Session 3

Session 4: Mindfulness of Schema Coping

Coping with problems

When confronted with (actual or seemingly) threatening and distressing situations, we instinctively respond in one of three ways: fight, flee, or freeze. These responses are typically automatic. As the body readies itself for action, the breath quickens and becomes more shallow, pupils dilate, and muscles tense or freeze up. The fight, flight, or freeze response is an important survival mechanism, especially when the choice of response is made consciously and is appropriate for the situation. However, more often than not, these reactions are unconscious, and our automatic pilot can sometimes do more harm than good.

Schemas and modes are linked to coping strategies as well, of which there are also three. When automatically triggered over long periods of time they can lead to lasting damage. The three schema-coping strategies are schema avoidance (fleeing), schema overcompensation (fighting), and schema surrender (freezing).

Schema avoidance involves efforts to steer clear of anything that might cause sadness, anger, or fear. This is achieved by seeking distractions or by avoiding situations that may trigger the respective schemas.

Schema overcompensation works by drowning out one's schemas by acting as if they hold no power or don't exist. For instance, people who dread failure often work extremely hard in order to ensure success, telling themselves that it's "a piece of cake."

In schema surrender, one is constantly on the lookout for information that can legitimize one's schemas. Everything about a situation is analyzed until some detail is found that confirms the schema in question. For instance, someone with the Mistrust and/or Abuse schema may not

126

accept another person's friendliness at face value. He will go to great lengths to identify a flaw in that person, something to support his schema.

The stories of Mark and Joanne illustrate how schema survival strategies frequently result in a constricted perspective while on automatic pilot.

> Mark went to bed late last night and worked overtime today. When he finally gets home at eight o'clock, his girlfriend confronts him and demands to know why he's late and didn't call. Mark feels annoyed. He was up all night working on a project for his boss, and today was another long and hectic day. Now he's finally home, but he still can't get a break because his girlfriend is being needy. Growing angrier by the minute, Mark scowls and drops his bag off in his study. Without a word he turns around and leaves the house.

This example shows Mark's Unrelenting Standards/Hypocritical schema being triggered. He believes his girlfriend is overly demanding, just like his boss and his job in general. Feeling unappreciated, Mark goes into Vulnerable Child mode and flees in Detached Protector mode. He has developed a kind of tunnel vision, which causes him to only see things that confirm his schema. Even though escaping feels like his best option in the short term, it may cause him to miss situations that could contradict his schemas. The fact is that he himself decided to work through the night and work overtime the following day. And though Mark interprets his girlfriend's inquiries as demands, she may just be worried about him working too hard, and misses spending time with him.

> Joanne has made a habit of bending over backwards to satisfy others while putting her own needs last. She avoids confrontation and rarely stands up for herself. One day a girlfriend calls

127

and points out that Joanne hasn't called in ages. This friend had recently been sick for a long time, during which Joanne took care of her. Joanne has only just begun to spend time and energy on herself again, so now she blows up, angrily accusing her friend of being selfish and ungrateful for all the support. The friend is shocked and apologizes. But then Joanne interprets the apology as proof that her friend really is just a parasite, which only makes her angrier.

Joanne is used to operating in Compliant Surrender mode, always adapting to the needs of others and exhibiting schema-confirming behavior. Her reactions to situations are based on Subjugation, Self-Sacrifice, and Approval-Seeking schemas, which keep her from standing up for herself. Whenever she does take a stand, she does so by blaming and shouting like the Angry Child—a schema over-compensation strategy. Joanne's intense reaction scares her girl-friend, whose apologies are then interpreted as confirmation of her schemas. But is Joanne's anger justified? In automatic pilot she forgets that her friend was actually very grateful for all the support. Her friend had gotten used to seeing her every day, and wonders why they haven't spoken for so long. In other words, she did not intend to accuse Joanne: she simply wanted to understand.

We all have schema-coping strategies, and each of us has a pre-ferred style. We will spend part of this session identifying your go-to strategy for schema survival by filling out the Schema Coping Questionnaire (Appendix III-E).

Your final score on this questionnaire will provide insight into your schema-coping strategies. Some participants receive identical scores for each strategy. If that happens to be the case, try to see if you scored a greater number of fives and sixes on one strategy in particular. If so, does that strategy seem to be your schema-coping strategy of choice? If neither of these approaches provides you with a clear answer, try to use mindfulness on a daily basis to discover your schema-coping strategies.

After you have identified your main personal schema-coping strategy, try to think of a past situation in which it may have played a role. See if you can come up with some other behaviors that illustrate how you act out your main coping strategy once your schemas are triggered.

Exercises

Exercise 4.1   Mindful Juggling[2]

- Stand on the floor with a ball in each hand. Be mindful of breathing. If and when you get distracted, by thoughts or otherwise, make a mental note of it and congratulate yourself for noticing. Then gently return your attention to the breath.
- Gradually expand your awareness to include the rest of your body. Feel both feet planted firmly on the floor. Notice how the juggling balls feel in your hands. Be mindful of your body. If you find that you are sidetracked, appreciate that you are mindful enough to notice. You can then use the breath as a stepping stone before returning to body mindfulness. Stay with your body for about two minutes before continuing to the next step.
- When you feel ready, throw the ball in your right hand upward and to the left—toward your left hand. Before it lands, toss the ball in your left hand up toward your right hand. Try to catch both balls. Now try again and keep trying until you get the hang of it. From time to time you will drop a ball, or the two balls will collide in midair. When that happens pay close attention to how you react. If you feel embarrassment, that feeling might be a sign that your Defectiveness/Shame schema has been triggered. If you start comparing yourself to others,

[2] This exercise is not included on the audio files.

129

admonishing yourself to keep up with the rest or even out-juggle them, then perhaps your Unrelenting Standards/Hypocritical schema or Demanding Parent mode has been activated. You can always start the process over by going back to mindful breathing, gradually expanding to the body, and back to juggling. Practice this for about 10 minutes.

Doing-mode

After completing the exercise in being-mode, ask yourself some questions about your observations. Closing your eyes or gazing at an imagined point in front of you may help you come up with answers.

- In what part of your body is your breath most noticeable? Does your breathing change in speed, depth, or location?
- What else do you notice happening? And what else?
- What is happening in your body? Which physical sensations are most present, and where? What kind of emotions do you feel? Which schemas and modes are being triggered?
- What do you feel like doing in order to get rid of your unpleasant feelings?

Below are the scripts for two audio file exercises that are not covered in the group.

Exercise 4.2   Cultivating Schema Mindfulness

Know when your schemas are operating. When you are uncomfortable, defensive, sad, impulsive, or worried, there is a good chance a schema has been triggered. The following exercise is designed to help you in those moments:

- Be mindful of your breathing for 30 to 60 seconds. Focus on your belly, chest, or wherever you feel your breath to be most present in this moment.
- Turn your attention to your internal experience. Be mindful of what is going on inside, anything related to whichever event, thought, or memory put you into your current state.
- Now come back to the breath for another 30 to 60 seconds. Be mindful of your belly, chest, or wherever you feel your breath to be most present in this moment.

Doing-mode

After completing the exercise above in *being-mode*, ask yourself some questions about your observations; what you noticed while being mindful. Closing your eyes or softly gazing at a spot in front of you may help you come up with answers.

- What kind of emotions are you experiencing? What are your strongest feelings right now? Schemas trigger specific emotions: the Abandonment/Instability schema elicits fear; the Emotional Deprivation schema brings sadness; the Mistrust and/or Abuse schema calls up anger. Which emotions are you experiencing? Are they familiar, do they remind you of past situations? How do they appear? How strong are they? Do these feelings change? Where do they reside in the body?
- What are you thinking? What are you telling yourself about what just happened? How are you interpreting your role in the situation? Or the other person's role? How are your thoughts trying to convince you that you did the right thing (like walking out, getting mad, or becoming distant)?
- Does this situation remind you of anything? What kind of memories are bubbling up? Have you had any similar

131

experiences before? Are you reminded of specific events from your past?

- How is the current situation similar to past ones? Did you behave the same way back then? Are you reminded of your schemas? If so, which ones? Now I will slowly count to three, after which you may open your eyes. Before returning to doing-mode, take a few moments to be mindful of your presence and of the world around you… 1… 2… 3.

Tip

- Whenever your attention trails off, focus on your breath. Be conscious of where you feel your body breathing. Once you've settled into that, you can expand your awareness to include whatever you were mindful of before losing your focus.
- You can also practice the exercise above by being mindful of which mode you are in. If you experience anger or negative thoughts toward yourself or others, then you may have been in Punitive Parent mode.
- While attempting to observe a situation with mindfulness, you may notice yourself losing focus quite a lot. You may also find your emotions getting stronger or weaker. All of this is normal. It just means your schemas are operating and are trying to get you sidetracked, so be aware that this can happen. When it does, take a second to reflect and then, with the caring and accepting attitude of the Healthy Adult, return to what you were doing.

Exercise 4.3 Getting to Know Your Schemas

- Be mindful of your breathing. Where do you feel your breath? Focus on that area. Maybe you are concentrating on the rhythm of your belly as it rises and falls with every breath. Or perhaps on the sensation of air rushing in and out of your nose. Find out where your experience of the breath is felt most strongly, and use it to be mindful of every breath.
- When you are ready, direct your attention towards the memory that is currently occupying your mind. Be mindful of all the bodily sensations, feelings, and thoughts you are having at this time.
- Now focus on your breath again. Be mindful of where it is most present in the body.

Doing-mode

After completing the exercise above in *being-mode*, ask yourself some questions about your observations; what you noticed while being mindful. Closing your eyes or softly gazing into space may help you come up with answers.

- Ask yourself whether you may have responded to the situation inappropriately. Would others have reacted the same way? What effect did your behavior have on the people around you? Did your actions intensify your emotions? Did you continue to overreact or did you withdraw? If your reaction, your thoughts, or feelings were somehow different or more intense than what you normally experience in Healthy Adult mode, then you have run into an active schema.
- What set off your schema? For instance, did you feel excluded from the group (Social Isolation/Alienation schema)? Did you feel as though somehow you're not as good as other

people, and that you always end up messing things up (Failure schema)? Perhaps you missed an appointment, forgot something at home, failed to be prepared, or went out and bought all kinds of unnecessary stuff (Insufficient Self-Control/Self-Discipline schema)? Each schema has its own triggers. If you can be mindful of how a situation unfolds— what you're feeling, thinking, and doing—then that can help you understand what may be triggering your schemas.

- What were you feeling at the time? Where in the body were your emotions most strongly felt? Each schema has an associated emotion and area in the body. Therefore you can learn how to recognize your schemas based on how and where your emotions manifest.
- What was going through your mind? For instance, were you worried about hurting someone by asking them for attention, or about infringing on their rights by standing up for yourself (Subjugation schema)?
- Where do your thoughts, feelings, and behaviors come from? If, for example, you felt unable to share with a friend that you feel vulnerable and hurt (Defectiveness/Shame schema), that may have roots in being bullied as a child for being timid or emotionally sensitive. I will now slowly count to three, after which you may open your eyes. Before returning to doing-mode, spend a few moments being mindful of your presence and the world around you... 1... 2... 3.

Homework

- Homework assignment: Everyday Mindfulness (Appendix III-A)
- Homework sheet: Cultivating Schema Mindfulness (Appendix III-C)
- Homework sheet: Writing a Summary (Appendix III-D)
- Audio files exercises: Body Scan (1.1), Cultivating Schema Mindfulness (4.2), Getting to Know Your Schemas (4.3)
- Read the text for Session 4

Session 5: Allowing and Accepting What Is

Reacting in Healthy Adult mode and Happy Child mode

Some situations can be difficult to handle with acceptance and mindfulness—especially when our schemas have been triggered and we are in a maladaptive mode. The automatic pilot can easily exacerbate situations, so it is important to stay vigilant of schemas and modes. It is equally important, however, to have an open and accepting point of view. In such a frame of mind the Healthy Adult and the Happy Child can successfully emerge. We all carry our Healthy Adult and Happy Child within us, but their development depends on life experience. If we grew up with inadequate role models to exemplify the Healthy Adult and give us healthy boundaries, then that part of us will not be well developed. If we spent much of our childhood on guard or taking care of someone, then we may be unaccustomed to feeling free and joyful, making it difficult to live in Happy Child mode.

The first step in leaving behind old schema thoughts and behaviors is to accept what is. Rather than responding with schema avoidance, surrender, or overcompensation, it is vital to face your loneliness and fear. Set boundaries on your anger and impulsiveness and uphold them with acceptance and determination. Permit yourself to make mistakes, not to always strive for perfection. Grant others the right to be imperfect and to respond in their own way, not how you want them to. Allow yourself to have fun. Do all these things with mindfulness, and recognize the fact that change takes time and may unfold differently from what you expect.

Frank is troubled by the following schemas: Mistrust and/or Abuse, Defectiveness/Shame, and Insufficient Self-Control/Self-Discipline. Life has taught him that people will inevitably betray or take advantage of him. Frank is at his brother's birthday party when he is approached by a stranger. Right away he finds himself doubting the man's intentions. "Why would anyone be interested

135

in me," he thinks. Frank notices that his rising anxiety has roused a thirst for beer, and this upsets him. Angrily he tells himself that "Drinking is no longer an option. It's time to stop making such a big deal out of things." He grows increasingly tense and gloomy as the conversation with the stranger becomes more awkward.

The above illustrates what can happen when a schema is triggered. All the ingredients for a failed interaction are there: the urge to drink, emotional demandingness, and an increasingly awkward conversation. When Frank becomes aware of his schemas and modes operating, the following events takes place:

Frank notices his schemas and modes being activated. He excuses himself and heads to the restroom, where he takes a few minutes of breathing space to mindfully observe what is going on. This gets him out automatic pilot and gives him a broader perspective of the situation. He shifts into Healthy Adult mode by reminding himself that the negative experiences of his past need not repeat themselves today; that it's okay to feel anxious and insecure; that it's fine to have a drink, as long as he respects his own boundaries. Frank returns to the party and joins the stranger. Their conversation gradually comes to life as mutual understanding and acceptance start to emerge.

Mindful interaction with loved ones

Discussions with partners, friends, and relatives can turn into never-ending arguments where both sides try to convince each other that one is right and the other wrong. This may take the form of calm conversation, or yelling and swearing, or even hitting and kicking. Another way that some people respond to conflict is by withdrawing, expressing displeasure through cold silence. Most arguments are not just about a current situation but involve sensitive areas related to past injury. Old wounds that were not necessarily inflicted by the present loved one, but reopened by current relationships nonetheless.

> Evelyn has been waiting for her boyfriend George since 6:00 this evening. She has prepared a romantic evening and put lots of effort into a special meal. She feels anxious as she paces back and forth, tidying up around the house. Her body feels tense. It's 6:45 and George still isn't home—even though he promised to be there by six. Grumbling to herself, her agitation slowly turns to anger. When George finally arrives at 7:30, Evelyn is so upset and disappointed that she blurts out "Forget it!" and heads off to the bedroom. George, who was asked to work late by his boss, is annoyed by Evelyn's behavior. First he was pressured into working overtime, and now his girlfriend is giving him a hard time as well. He follows her into the bedroom and an argument ensues.

At first glance it appears that Evelyn is simply upset about a broken promise, and that George feels overwhelmed by his responsibilities toward others. However, there is more going on. After Evelyn and George have calmed down, they take some time to mindfully discuss what happened and which of their schemas were triggered. It emerges that Evelyn felt blown off (Emotional Deprivation), and George felt obliged to cater to others yet again (Subjugation).

If you and your partner, friend, or relative take time out during an argument and allow each other to mindfully observe which schemas have been triggered, you can avoid escalation of the conflict. Furthermore, assuming the perspective of the Healthy Adult will improve your ability to challenge your schemas. Your past experiences that led to the formation of your schemas do not have to be repeated; recognition of this fact enables you to navigate your way around them.

Exercises

Exercise 5.1 Three Minute Schema Mindfulness

Observing, opening up, and allowing your experience to happen will (eventually) lead to a feeling of acceptance toward yourself and other people. But being mindful of self and others is more easily said than done. Your way of perceiving the world has been shaped by schemas for so long that alternate perspectives are basically out of reach, which means that automatic pilot regularly and all too easily gains the upper hand. Mindfulness is the key to stepping out of automatic pilot. Mindful living, without immediate reaction, opens up room for more conscious and volitional actions.

- Be mindful of your breathing. Pay attention to each inhalation and exhalation. Notice where you feel your breath moving around the body. Expand your awareness from the breath to the thoughts appearing and disappearing in your mind.
- Allow your thoughts to arise without censoring them. The more tolerant you are of your thoughts, the more you can accept their presence inside the safe confines of your head, the closer you can get to your schemas. Let each thought rise up and study it like a new acquaintance. What it looks or sounds like doesn't matter. No one is judging or condemning you. These are your thoughts appearing in your head. If any emotions come up, allow them to happen in just the same way.
- Stay aware of your breath as you watch all your thoughts emerge in the foreground and dissolve into the background.

Doing-mode

After completing the exercise above, ask yourself some questions about your observations; what you noticed while being mindful. Closing your eyes or softly gazing into space may help you come up with answers.

- Did your thoughts include any objective facts? Did any emotions present themselves? What else did you experience? Did you recognize any schemas? Did you identify your mode?
- Be mindful of your breathing. You are going to address yourself with a mild and gentle voice. Try to be the Healthy Adult and speak to the schemas you observed before. Approach any feelings of abandonment, abuse, or loneliness with kindness and compassion. Be calm yet resolved in setting boundaries on your anger and impulsiveness. Let go of your demands, and of your need to control or punish yourself and others. If you catch yourself trailing off or getting caught in the stream of thoughts and emotions produced by your schemas, be gentle but firm in guiding your attention back towards the breath. I will now slowly count to three, upon which you may open your eyes. Before jumping back into doing-mode, take a few moments to become fully present within yourself and your current environment... 1... 2... 3.

Exercise 5.2   Mindful Acceptance of Self and Other[3]

Along with the mindfulness exercises designed to improve your ability to recognize schemas and modes, it is also important to learn and practice dealing with thoughts that challenge or contradict your schemas. This can be very difficult. It is much easier to spot (negative) situations that support your schemas and

[3] This exercise is not included on the audio files.

modes than those that don't. Someone with the Mistrust and/or Abuse schema will quickly conclude that people are dishonest and untrustworthy when they see a cashier slipping some of the change into her pocket. But this same person will quickly forget that a friend in whom she confided with private information did in fact keep those issues to herself. To practice countering schema avoidance strategies, the following exercise will involve mindful reflection on thoughts that are actually positive and constructive— thoughts that invalidate schemas. Examples can be drawn from simple situations in life, such as the time you said "No" to someone and they respected your decision, or even complimented you for standing your ground (this would invalidate Self-Sacrifice and Approval-Seeking schemas). A few examples of positive, constructive, and accepting thoughts related to various schemas are listed below.

Examples of more positive and accepting approaches to schemas

- Emotional Deprivation: "Although I often feel as though others don't support me and neglect my emotional needs, there have also been times when people did support me and provided the approval I need. Whenever I need attention and encouragement, I can simply ask for it in a friendly, calm, and straightforward way. There is no need to demand immediate satisfaction. There will always be people around who love me."
- Unrelenting Standards/Hypocritical: "I have a right to make mistakes. I can only do my best, and that's plenty. Others are allowed to make mistakes too. If nobody made mistakes, we would be no different from robots—deprived of our humanity."
- Insufficient Self-Control/Self-Discipline: "Even though I don't like doing chores, it is important to fulfill my duties so

I don't run into problems down the road. Expecting short-term rewards isn't good for me. I will always benefit in the long term somehow. Even if I have to wait."

Examples of more positive and accepting approaches to modes

- Compliant Surrender: "I don't always need to adapt to others. I have my own needs and desires. People may not always like it when I stand up for myself, but that's okay. Most people will find it completely normal if I value my own needs and desires."
- Detached Protector: "By shutting myself off from the world, I am hurting myself. A better way to protect myself in vulnerable moments is to reach out to people I trust, to let them know I'm hurt. That way I'll be more likely to receive emotional support and to feel better."
- Self-Aggrandizer: "It is good to feel proud of my achievements, and once in a while it can be okay to think of myself as being better at something than others. But it's important to stay grounded in reality. Being better at one thing doesn't make me a superior person. Other people also have a need to be recognized for their achievements. I can set the example by giving others the opportunity to feel proud."

Doing-mode

- Based on your primary schemas and modes, come up with some additional positive, accepting thoughts that work for you. Write down three constructive ideas for each of your schemas and modes. Feel free to ask a significant other to help you formulate some positive and helpful thoughts.

Tip

- Some people feel the need to put their thoughts into writing. They may require a safe environment to do so. Pick a time and place where you can simply be yourself, like your bedroom or study. Before you start, consciously decide where you plan to write and where you will store your writings.
- Don't force yourself to write every day. Make the decision of whether or not to write (or to practice any other activity requiring presence of mind) a mindful one. Be extra mindful about your decision if you have worries on your mind.
- Don't write as if you are addressing someone. Doing so might restrict your freedom of thought, causing you to hold back or censor your own words. You want to be free to let everything in and out.

Homework

- Homework assignment: Everyday Mindfulness (Appendix III-A)
- Homework sheet: Complete Five-Facet M Questionnaire (Appendix III-B)
- Homework sheet: Cultivating Schema Mindfulness (Appendix III-C)
- Homework sheet: Writing a Summary (Appendix III-D)
- Audio file exercises: Body Scan (1.2), Three Minute Schema Mindfulness (5.1)
- Exercise: Mindful Acceptance of Self and Other (5.2)
- Read the text for Session 5

Session 6: Schemas: Fact or Fiction?

The schemas we develop over the course of our lives determine how we perceive the world, other people, ourselves, our bodies, our feelings, and our actions. Childhood neglect teaches us that people worry about their own needs but not enough about ours, and so we learn not to count on others. Those of us with Mistrust and/or Abuse schemas construe ambiguous situations as threatening, or we interpret physical sensations, such as butterflies in the stomach or tension in the neck, as signs of impending doom. Sadness can leave us feeling lonely and empty.

The past seems to haunt us through our schemas. But experiencing the same powerful emotions that we did in the past does not necessarily mean that we are experiencing those same situations. It is vital to remember that schemas are only thoughts—and thoughts are not facts. They are merely ideas; clusters of words that we ourselves put together. If we make the mistake of seeing thoughts as truth, we become prone to the kinds of scenarios described below.

- Someone who is always judging herself and others, who is strict, demanding, and punitive, will constantly struggle with feelings of anger and resentment.
- Someone who sees the world in black and white, who only thinks in extremes, will consistently feel disappointed and unhappy.
- Someone who always expects perfection, who cannot tolerate error or pain, will repeatedly face failure, inadequacy, and shame. The truth is that perfection is not required for effective functioning or for feeling valued.
- A person who is always apologizing will feel pressured to defend herself, to adapt to others, and to bow down to them. In reality, getting acceptance from others does not require us to excuse our every action.
- Someone who is always explaining and justifying his every action forgets that we can't always respond to criticism. Nor do we need to.

In spite of our best efforts to avoid criticism, no one goes through life without it.

- Blaming other people when things don't go our way only serves to push them out of our lives. And pointing fingers doesn't make us any less critical of our own shortcomings. The truth is that there is no such thing as a perfect human being. Everyone makes mistakes.

- Always expecting the worst possible outcome is not a belief based on reality. Yes, the future is uncertain, but that does not mean the worst will come to pass.

- Feeling tense, sad, angry, or afraid does not always mean there is reason for that feeling. For example, assuming that your anxiety is related to some impending danger will only make you more anxious. It will cause you to "freeze" (not knowing what to do), instead of having the presence of mind required to face potential problems.

- Feeling a constant urge to be productive only leads to stress and frustration. Relatively few things in life truly require us to act; for everything else we have a choice.

- Making mountains out of molehills when things go wrong tends to result in feelings of failure and defeat. Yes, things don't always go our way, but that is not always a disaster.

- Going on the defensive when criticized usually means that we feel personally attacked; as though our very identities have been assaulted. However, others may simply be offering constructive criticism. In any case, it is always up to us to decide how we react.

- Some people respond to unpleasant events by recalling other negative events in the past. This way of thinking filters out the positive. People lose sight of pleasant experiences in the past and present, and their lives and future expectations become tainted by negativity.

- Although we consider our view of the world to be accurate, it can often be significantly distorted. This is because situations are always interpreted through the lens of personal experience, or in other words, on the basis of schemas and modes. Pure objectivity is impossible, which makes misinterpretation an inevitable consequence of being a human being.

Remember the following:

- Schemas are not facts. They are negative suggestions. Schemas are stories that we ourselves have written and we ourselves can change.
- Many of the things that trouble us are issues everyone regularly deals with. Negative events are often not nearly as significant as our schemas make them out to be.
- Try to let go of endlessly striving for success, victory, and perfection. It keeps you from being relaxed and enjoying interactions with other people.
- Schemas come and go. Keep in mind that they appear and disappear automatically. Avoid spontaneous reactions by being mindful and taking your time to decide on a response.
- Schemas are like self-fulfilling prophecies. The first step toward change is mindfully recognizing patterns in your thoughts, feelings, and actions (as well as those of others). Once you let go of your allegiance to your schemas, you can begin to break through the self-destructive behaviors that sustain them.

From intent to action

A fraction of a second elapses between our decision to act and the action that follows. We are usually unaware of the brief moment between forming our intention to act and then performing our intended action. It may seem like our response is automatic, but it is, in fact, unconscious.

Veronica and a neighbor are in the apartment elevator. She notices the young man dropping his cigarette butt on the floor. Veronica finds this unacceptable; people should always dispose of their trash appropriately (Unrelenting Standards/Hypocritical schema).

She is reluctant to address the young man, as she fears any form of confrontation (Subjugation schema), yet she decides to address the issue. Politely, though with a hint of sternness, Veronica says: "Would you please pick up your cigarette and throw it in the trash?" The neighbor responds sharply, telling her to pick it up and throw it away herself. Veronica immediately apologizes. When they leave the elevator the cigarette is still on the floor.

This situation presents both Veronica and her neighbor with several opportunities for mindfulness; moments in which they could have reflected on intent, rather than leaping into action. As a result of their unconscious reacting, both were left feeling uncomfortable while the cigarette butt was left on the floor. Which moments of potential mindfulness can you identify in this example? Ask yourself the same question in respect to a situation from your past.

Exercises

Exercise 6.1   Walking with Mindful Intent

The walking exercise from Session 3 can help you develop awareness of your intent; that is, the idea or goal that precedes an associated action. This version of the exercise places even more emphasis on mindful intent, allowing you to pause and reflect on your options instead of unconsciously reacting. This exercise can be carried out indoors or outside.

- Find a place with plenty of room to walk.
- Stand with your knees slightly bent to allow for some bounce in your legs. Keep your feet about 10–15 cm apart. Let your arms hang freely by your sides and maintain a softly focused gaze ahead of you.

- Focus your attention on the soles of your feet, and feel the contact with the ground. Notice the weight of your body passing through your legs and feet into the ground. You are about to bend your knees, but first, contemplate the emerging intention to bend your knees. Then bend them a number of times, sensing the movement of your legs and feet, and making sure to reflect on your intent before every action.
- For each of the following movements, be mindful of your intention to move, and of each subsequent action as it occurs.
- When you are ready, shift the weight of your body to your right leg. Notice the new sensation in your legs and feet, as your right leg now supports most of your weight, and your left leg feels lighter.
- For each of the following movements, be mindful of your intention to move, and of each subsequent action as it occurs.
- Raise your left heel off the floor and feel the slight strain in your calf muscles.
- Slowly roll your left foot up until only your toes touch the floor. Be mindful of the changing sensations in your legs and feet.
- Now raise your left foot and carefully move it forwards.
- Be mindful of the feeling of your leg and foot gliding through the air, before you place your heel back on the floor in front of you.
- Let the rest of your foot come down as you gradually shift your weight to the left side of your body.
- Now sense how your left leg and foot get heavier as you prepare to take the next step with your right.
- For each of the following movements, be mindful of your intention to move, and of each subsequent action as it occurs.
- Once you are supported by your left leg, raise your right foot off the floor and slowly move it forwards.
- Be mindful of the changing sensations in your legs and feet while moving forward.

- Be mindful of your right heel as it makes contact with the floor.
- Once your right foot is firmly planted on the floor, shift your weight to that side of the body.
- Stay aware of the continuously changing sensations in both legs and feet.
- For each of the following movements, be mindful of your intention to move, and of each subsequent action as it occurs.
- Begin walking around.
- Be mindful of each step, giving unbroken attention to the feeling of your leg muscles moving and your soles touching the floor.
- For each of the following movements, be mindful of your intention to move, and of each subsequent action as it occurs.
- If and when you turn around, try to appreciate the complex sequence of movements your body makes while changing direction, and then continue walking.
- For each of the following movements, be mindful of your intention to move, and of each subsequent action as it occurs.
- Keep moving back and forth, being as mindful as you can of the sensation in your legs and feet.
- Maintain your softly focused gaze as you look straight head.
- When you notice your attention drawing away from the experience of walking, go back to being mindful of your legs and feet.
- Just as you used your breath in seated meditation, use the contact between your feet and the floor as an anchor. This contact will ground you in the here and now.
- Continue walking in this way for 10 to 15 minutes, or longer if you wish.

When you begin the walking exercise, start off slowly so you can get used to being mindful. Once you get the hang of it, pick up to whatever speed is comfortable for you. However, if you feel rushed or restless when starting off, try launching into it at a slightly less rapid pace. Gradually reduce your speed as you begin to calm down.

Participant Workbook

Exercise 6.2   Letting Go of Schemas

This exercise can be carried out after exercises that involve painful experiences (such as Exercise 3.2), but it is also useful for confronting highly emotional situations in daily life. The exercise calls for an open, curious frame of mind, while observing thoughts, feelings, and actions with renewed attention.

Pay close attention when experiencing a (strong) emotional reaction. You may become furious after hearing a negative remark, or very unhappy after someone special has gone away. Alternatively, you might experience an emotion that does not fit with the situation at all, for instance, feeling hurt when others would normally get angry. Or perhaps you might (suddenly) feel nothing at all.

Immediate emotional reactions are noticeable in the moment or after the fact. Pay attention to what is happening around you at the time; be mindful of your thoughts, feelings, and behavior. The more you practice mindfulness in emotional moments, the more your ability to "catch" these reactions will improve.

Becoming aware of changes in your thoughts, feelings, and behavior disengages the automatic pilot. Emotions (gradually) cease to spiral out of control and no longer spontaneously disappear. Thoughts slow down as you begin to notice them coming and going, accepting their presence in your mind. You learn to recognize how certain thoughts, feeling, and behaviors belong to situations from your past, but are no longer appropriate. By cultivating renewed awareness and nonjudgmental mindfulness of your emotions, thoughts, and actions, you will notice an increased ability to make conscious decisions.

For instance, when feeling angry or sad, find a place to sit down and focus on your breath. Where in the body do you feel your breath? Expand your attention from that point to the rest of your body, enveloping the emotion you are experiencing.

149

Return to the breath every time your emotions swallow-up your attention and get you distracted. See your feelings as a dark cloud passing overhead; no intervention is required. Just be mindful of what you feel, do, see, hear, and smell. Be mindful of your environment, while keeping your attention anchored in the part of your body where your emotion is felt.

I will now slowly count to three, after which you may open your eyes. Before going back to doing-mode, spend a few moments being mindful of yourself and your current surroundings... 1... 2... 3.

Homework

- Homework assignment: Everyday Mindfulness (Appendix III-A)
- Homework sheet: Cultivating Schema Mindfulness (Appendix III-C)
- Homework sheet: Writing a Summary (Appendix III-D)
- Audio file exercises: Body Scan (1.2), Letting Go of Schemas (6.2)
- Exercise: Walking with Mindful Intent (6.1)
- Read the text for Session 6

Session 7: Caring For Yourself Through the Healthy Adult and the Happy Child

The previous sessions have revolved around the experience of physical sensations, emotions, and thoughts as a foundation for developing schema and mode mindfulness. This session highlights the Healthy Adult and the Happy Child modes. We will reflect on the images of the Healthy Adult and the Happy Child, determining their presence in the body and exploring the experiences they bring up. No one will have the same experience. Some may find themselves unable to picture themselves as a Healthy Adult; others may realize they never knew real happiness as a child. Various emotions and bodily sensations may arise during this session, or none may occur at all. The key, as always, is to practice observing these experiences mindfully.

Whenever Natalie makes a mistake, this triggers her Punitive mode which is linked to the Unrelenting Standards/Hypocritical schema. She scolds and insults herself. During the "Mindfulness of the Healthy Adult and the Happy Child" exercise, in which Natalie becomes annoyed with herself for her inability to picture herself as the Healthy Adult, the same reactive pattern emerges. Her brooding and self-criticism causes her to miss the examples given out on how a Healthy Adult might behave. During the follow-up discussion, Natalie realizes that she missed the examples and becomes even more upset. The trainer asks her to pause and reflect on those feelings; Natalie notices her anger turning to sadness. Being mindful helps her see herself from a more mild and gentle point of view.

Exercises

Exercise 7.1   Mindfulness of the Healthy Adult and the Happy Child

This mindfulness exercise will allow you to observe your Healthy Adult and Happy Child. It provides a way to become more conscious of the healthy aspects of yourself, those on which you can depend in challenging situations.

- Sit down in a chair with a straight back. Do not recline but keep your back straight.
- Let your back find an upright, relaxed, and dignified posture.

- Rest your feet flat on the floor.
- Close your eyes.
- Become aware of the feeling of contact and pressure on the parts of your body touching your seat and the floor. Take a few minutes to examine these sensations, just like in the Body Scan exercise.
- Focus on a part of your body where you can feel your breath. Notice the movement of your belly as you inhale and exhale, or focus on the feeling of air rushing in and out of your nose with every breath. Mindfully observe your body where the experience of breathing is most noticeable, allowing you to stay focused on the breath.
- Now focus your attention on the image of yourself as the Healthy Adult. Reflect on how the Healthy Adult within you can offer comfort and protection, with kindness and composure; how it is capable of witnessing strict, punitive, or angry moods from a gentle, mild frame of mind. You can also contemplate the part of your Healthy Adult that sets healthy boundaries for yourself and others in your environment; and to ensure that it does so in a calm and friendly way.
- Whenever you notice your attention being sidetracked from the Healthy Adult, gently remind yourself that you are doing well to be so mindful. Remember that everyone gets distracted; the fact that you recognized this simply provides a new opportunity to become mindful of your Healthy Adult. Use your breath as a stepping stone to the Healthy part of you if necessary.
- Return to the breath as the focus of your attention. Be mindful of inhaling and exhaling, and of the natural variation in that process. Train your attention on the start of each breath and hold it there until the end, maintaining awareness of every inhalation and exhalation. Notice

152

whenever you get sidetracked, returning your attention to the breath.

- Now focus on the image of yourself as a Happy Child. Notice how safe and secure the child feels. Notice the self-confidence of the Happy Child. The feeling of being embraced by the people around him or her. The knowledge that he or she is free to pursue independence in a healthy way.

- Come back to the breath as point of focus. Staying mindful of each and every breath, ask yourself what the Healthy Adult and Happy Child will need in order to express themselves in the future; to be more present and aware. If you notice yourself trailing off, gently take note and then return to the breath. Reflect on what the Healthy Adult and Happy Child will need for the future.

Doing-mode

Reflecting on the previous exercise, go over the kinds of experiences you observed; examine the things you noticed while mindful. Coming up with answers may be easier with your eyes closed, or while keeping a softly focused gaze on an imagined point.

- What does the Healthy Adult look like? Where in your body do you feel the Healthy Adult to be most present? What else do you notice about the Healthy Adult?
- What does your Happy Child look like? Where in the body do you feel the Healthy Child to be most present?
- I will now slowly count to three, after which you may open your eyes. Before going back to doing-mode, take a moment to become aware of your presence and the world around you... 1... 2... 3.

Preparing for the future: doing-mode

In Session 5 we covered how you can respond to situations from the perspectives of the Healthy Adult and the Happy Child; how to handle schemas being triggered; and how to observe and become more mindful of events with greater kindness and acceptance. An important part of looking after yourself is to be aware of potential pitfalls (such as negative thoughts and behaviors), but also of your positive thoughts and the things that you do well. When your schemas are running and you are stuck in a mode, things that go wrong tend to swallow up your attention. Only the thoughts and perceptions that are consistent with our schema or mode make it into your conscious experience.

> Two weeks ago Richard pulled a muscle during a game of soccer, and now he is in a great deal of pain. His doctor ordered him to rest and avoid playing soccer for at least three months. Richard is very upset about this. Furthermore, he hasn't heard from any of his soccer buddies since last week, and he is beginning to suspect that they are neglecting him. That he is not important enough to visit. Reflecting on the situation, Richard's anger grows. But what he fails to realize is that his soccer friends are very worried about him, and he forgets that they came to visit him last week. Moreover, a couple of his buddies emailed and texted him just yesterday, telling him they would come and visit soon.

Sometimes our emotions take up all of our attention, so that we lose track of the positive memories and experiences we have had. In this session you will practice mindfulness of the Healthy Adult, focusing on letting go of schema-based thinking.

Exercise 7.2 involves being mindful in doing-mode. You will investigate which of your thoughts and actions are supportive of your schema, and which ones contradict or invalidate it. An example using Richard's situation is provided below.

Richard has (among others) the Emotional Deprivation schema. He writes down the following.

Schema 1: Emotional Deprivation
Three schema-surrendering thoughts are:
"My friends don't care enough about me to come and visit."
"I probably annoyed my doctor by bothering him with my injury."
"Right when I need my closest people to be there for me, they are nowhere to be found."

Three schema-surrendering behaviors are:
"Not responding to concerned emails and messages from my friends."
"Giving my girlfriend the cold shoulder."
"Telling everyone that nobody gives a hoot about me."

Three schema-invalidating thoughts are:
"My soccer team must care about me, because they came to check up on me last week."
"My soccer buddies do think about me, because some of them sent me emails and messages just yesterday."
"My girlfriend brought me to the doctor, and she always takes good care of me."

Three schema-negating behaviors are:
"Inviting my team over for a good time; enjoying their company."
"Actually asking my friends if they thought about me."
"Taking my girlfriend out for dinner and a movie; reminding myself that she is always there for me in rough times."

Exercise 7.2   Preparing for the Future[4]

Try to recognize which of your thoughts and behaviors are schema-confirming and which ones are schema-contradicting. Fill in the following items for each of your three highest-scoring schemas:

Schema 1
Three schema-surrendering thoughts are:

_____
_____
_____

Three schema-surrendering behaviors are:

_____
_____
_____

Schema 2
Three schema-surrendering thoughts are:

_____
_____
_____

Three schema-surrendering behaviors are:

_____
_____
_____

Schema 3
Three schema-surrendering thoughts are:

_____
_____
_____

[4]   This exercise is not included on the audio files.

Three schema-surrendering behaviors are:

_____

_____

_____

Fill in the following items for each of your three highest-scoring schemas:

Schema 1
Three schema-contradicting thoughts are:

_____

_____

_____

Three schema-contradicting behaviors are:

_____

_____

_____

Schema 2
Three schema-contradicting thoughts are:

_____

_____

_____

Three schema-contradicting behaviors are:

_____

_____

_____

Schema 3
Three schema-contradicting thoughts are:

_____

_____

_____

Three schema-contradicting behaviors are:

_____

_____

_____

Exercise 7.3   What Do the Healthy Adult and the Happy Child Need?[5]

Consider what you may need in order to respond in Healthy Adult mode and Happy Child mode. Bear in mind that the Healthy Adult supports, understands, and protects the Vulnerable mode, and it sets boundaries for the Demanding Parent, Angry Child, and Impulsive Child modes. The Happy Child feels loved, surrounded by loved ones and has the confidence to function independently.

What and/or who do I need in order to function in Healthy Adult mode:

_____

_____

_____

What and/or who do I need in order to function in Happy Child mode:

_____

_____

_____

[5]   This exercise is not included on the audio files.

The following text is taken from an audio file exercise that was not covered in the group.

Exercise 7.4 Mindfulness of Schemas as Mere Thoughts

Try to step out of your automatic pilot. Be mindful of your surroundings, other people, and yourself. What do you notice? How do you experience the world around you? How do you see others? What are you feeling? In what part of your body are those feelings most present? Do you perceive the world and the people around you as threatening, flawed, or cold and distant? Do you feel unhappy, angry, or extremely vulnerable? The instant you recognize a schema being triggered, take a moment to breath and become aware of your thoughts, feelings, and bodily sensations. This will provide clues about which schema has been triggered. Taking some breathing space provides more freedom of choice. Are you overreacting or avoiding, or are you experiencing the world from a surrendering frame of mind? Many of these experiences can be signs pointing to schema activation.

Understand that schemas are only thoughts; they are ideas about reality. Those ideas are not necessarily correct, nor do they accurately represent the world or the truth. You can challenge your schemas by reminding yourself that they are only one perspective of reality; like a pair of colored glasses that distort your perception of the world. Try removing your schema glasses to find out what else you can see. Make an effort to observe as much as possible; all the things you would not have seen or felt otherwise.

Be lenient with the way you have learned to see the world through your schema glasses. It is a logical consequence of the experiences of your past. When observing your schemas with acceptance, try to notice the change in your experience. See the things that were not visible through your schema glasses, even though they were there all along. Be mindful and curious about all the facts that make your schemas increasingly unnecessary.

I will now slowly count to three, after which you may open your eyes. Before jumping back into doing-mode, spend a moment in mindfulness of yourself and your present environment... 1... 2... 3.

Tip: Mindfully Handling Your Schemas

- Whenever a schema is triggered, try to come up with at least one positive response that opposes or delays your typical automatic reaction.
- Challenge your automatic thoughts (that is, your schemas). Have you carefully considered all the facts about your current situation? Is there anything you are (purposefully) ignoring? Can you (or others) identify any details that contradict your schema? Can you recall any past situations that showed your schema to be incorrect? If necessary, ask someone to help you think of situations or facts that might contradict the presently triggered schema.
- Focus on your breathing. Do not allow yourself to be consumed by (painful) emotions and thoughts. Be mindful of the situation in which your schema was triggered. Do you have a moment to distance yourself from whatever affected you? Perhaps you can briefly withdraw from the situation or go for a short walk.
- Try to respond positively whenever a schema is activated. For example, if you feel cheated and you notice an urge to get defensive, try to identify the emotion or painful sensation you are experiencing. Take your time. Come back to the breath whenever you notice an automatic reaction popping up. Keep practicing.

Homework

- Homework assignment: Everyday Mindfulness (Appendix III-A)
- Homework sheet: Complete Five-Facet M Questionnaire (Appendix III-B)
- Homework sheet: Cultivating Schema Mindfulness (Appendix III-C)
- Homework sheet: Writing a Summary (Appendix III-C)
- Audio files exercises: Body Scan (1.2), Mindful of the Healthy Adult and the Happy Child (7.1), Mindfulness of Schemas as Mere Thoughts (7.4)
- Exercise: Preparing for the Future (7.2), What Do the Healthy Adult and the Happy Child Need? (7.3)
- Read the text for Session 7

Session 8: The Future

Schemas and modes in the future

Daily mindfulness of schemas, modes, and the automatic pilot habit is a valuable practice for both the present and the future. It may take a long time for schema- and mode-related patterns of behavior to lose their influence, and to replace the tendency to operate in automatic pilot with continuous mindful reactions.

Over the course of the last seven sessions, you have acquired knowledge and skills concerning the operation of your schemas and modes, as well as the workings of your automatic pilot. For each session you have written a summary of the most important subjects that were covered. You can continue to refer to those summaries in the future. Select a number of exercises that you can see yourself practicing on a regular basis over the coming months and years. It will work to your advantage to prepare a plan of action, so now is a great moment to decide on some set days and times in the week that you can devote to mindfulness exercises. Make sure you write them down. Be mindful of the fact that, whatever the future may hold, you can always rely on your breath as an anchor to the present moment. The decision to avoid automatic pilot, to react with mindfulness of schemas and modes, is always yours to make. Your vigilance of the influence of schemas and modes is something you can bring into your social interactions as well. Mindfulness can function as a guide to inform the way you think, speak, and act around other people.

Mindfully interacting with loved ones in the future

Whenever disagreement arises between you and someone close, find a suitable moment for mindful reflection. Sometimes you or the other person may need a brief time-out; a dedicated break that allows you both to become mindful of the body, emotions, and whichever schemas and modes may have been triggered. A deliberate pause also permits (strong) emotions to subside. Once you have taken some time to calmly contemplate your experience, you can return to doing-mode in order to continue observing your experience through the following questions:

1. What are you feeling? Where in your body are your emotions most pronounced? Is there a knot in your stomach? Tension in your neck and/or shoulders? Trembling in your arms or legs? Are you jumping from one emotion to another, or are your feelings jumbled together? Do they remind you of a similar experience from the past?
2. What are you thinking? Try giving your feelings a "voice." Pay attention to what might be feeding your emotions. Which thoughts may be aggravating them—or holding them off. You might become aware of, for example, the following kind of thinking: "I'm always left to my own devices. No one notices me." What is it about your current situation that triggers such thoughts?
3. What are you doing in this situation? What mood are you in? Are your moods alternating? Do they cycle rapidly or do they linger? What does your mood make you feel like doing? What have you already done?

After taking a mindful break from the argument with your loved one, ask yourself what you gained. Did you gain insight into the schemas and modes influencing the situation? Are you open to discussing what happened? Even if you haven't fully understood which of your buttons were pushed, going over it together can help to identify triggers and strengthen your relationship. Once you feel confident of your ability to address the situation with mindfulness of yourself and the other, set about the following actions:

1. Agree upon a moment when you can meet under calmer conditions. Make sure you both have enough time and attention for a conversation.
2. Explain to the other person which of your schemas were activated, and in which modes you ended up. Identify which of their actions triggered your schemas. Speak from the first-person perspective, noting that you are not attacking them, but simply explaining how their behavior affected you. Try to show them specifically how your schemas were activated. For example: "I've noticed that, when people don't keep their promises or break the rules, my Emotional Deprivation schema gets triggered. This schema makes me feel neglected and rejected, to which I respond by becoming overly demanding or spiteful. That is what happened after you showed up late. I felt as though you had forgotten me—neglected me—just like my parents used to do. They were always off arguing and only worrying about themselves."
3. Invite your loved one to describe their own experience. What schemas and modes did they end up in? How did your reactions affect them? Stay mindful and inquisitive during their response, and realize that everything you hear might help both of you to deal with schemas more effectively in the future.
4. Discuss how schema triggers can be avoided in the future, and how you can disconnect from schemas once they are up and running. How can you respond to one another's needs with mutual respect? How will you confront schema triggers as a team? Lastly, is there anything more to discuss regarding the current situation?

5. Be patient if the same patterns continue to happen and they still activate your schemas and modes. You can't expect them to disappear overnight. Also recognize that people grow at different rates. Perhaps you will experience considerable change in a short amount of time, but your partner may need more practice—or vice versa. The important thing is to continue to be mindful and curious about each situation with your loved one. Try to learn something new from every encounter.

6. Your loved one might be interested in trying some mindfulness exercises. If so, find an exercise you can both value and enjoy, and practice it together. Alternatively, if no exercise can be agreed upon, choose different ones to carry out separately. Either way is fine; working on a more mindful relationship is challenging enough as it is.

Exercises

Exercise 8.1   Mindfulness of Yourself as Child and Adult

Being-mode part 1

*   Sit up straight with your back against the back of a chair. Place both feet on the floor. Close your eyes and focus on your breath. Concentrate on where in your body you are most aware of inhaling and exhaling. If you find yourself getting distracted by thoughts or images, compliment yourself for noticing. Then softly reorient yourself toward the breath.

Doing-mode part 1

After completing the experience-focused exercise above, close your eyes (or gaze at an imagined point), stay focused on the breath, and calmly transition to a doing-oriented mode of mindfulness.

- Form an image of a place where you feel safe and secure. Perhaps there is someone with you, a person you love and trust. Think of a warm and pleasant space with a relaxed atmosphere. Wherever this place may be, let it be somewhere you feel safe, protected, and supported. Where you are free to be yourself, with no need to impress anyone or pretend to be stronger or better than you actually are at this moment in time.

- Start to observe any images, thoughts, or feelings that emerge. Let your awareness come from a place of inner wisdom and acceptance, without judgment of your experiences. Know that you can always come back to your breath and the safe space you imagined. At this time you may become aware of material from the time your schemas and modes were formed. You might discover a connection between the pattern of your emotional reactions and the way they originally developed. Remember that your breath is always there to lead you back to that safe place in the present.

- Choose (an aspect of) an experience to examine from close up. If you become overwhelmed by the feelings or thoughts that arise, consider returning to it later, and move on to something else for now. For example, if someone who disappointed you comes to mind, give that image in your mind your full attention. Imagine that this person now approaches you with a mindful and open attitude. That they would like to listen to you, to be there for you and your needs.

- Allow yourself to honestly and plainly express whatever it is you need to say to this person. Do not hold back. Reflect on what you would really like to tell them, and then say it. Understand what it is you need from this person and explain it to them. Maybe you want them to be there for you more often; maybe you need them to be more sensitive, attentive, and caring. Use your own words to explain your needs.

- Your breath can be your anchor, a firm foundation enabling you to speak with calm and composure. Notice how this person is giving you their full attention. Recognize how they value the fact that you are openly expressing your thoughts, feelings, and needs.
- In your mind, let this person say exactly what it is you need to hear from them. Whatever feels good for you to hear.

Being-mode part 2

- After letting this person communicate their support to you, turn your attention to the breath once more. Be mindful of the sensation of air entering and leaving your body.
- Be mindful of any physical sensations. Be aware of the presence, or absence, of any thoughts and emotions.
- Try not to judge or censor any of your thoughts, feelings, and bodily sensations as they enter your awareness. Observe them as if they are utterly fresh. If you find yourself slipping out of mindfulness and falling into automatic pilot, acknowledge this. Take note of it and then gently return to your previous object of attention.
- Now come back to your breath. Notice it in your belly, chest, throat, mouth, or nose. Wherever you can be mindful of breathing without feeling a need to change it.

Doing-mode part 2

After completing the exercise above in being-mode, ask yourself some questions about your observations; what you noticed in your mindful state. Closing your eyes or softly gazing into space may help you come up with answers.

- Where do you feel your breath? What are you sensing in your body? Which emotions do you feel?

166

- How was it to let your thoughts and mental images arise without judgment?
- How did it feel to mindfully express your needs to another person? What did you become aware of? Which emotions? Where in the body?
- How was it to have this person listen to you and tell you what you need to hear? Which experiences did it bring into awareness? Which emotions? Where in the body? I will now slowly count to three; at three, you may open your eyes. Before switching to doing-mode, take a few moments to become aware of yourself and your present environment... 1... 2... 3.

Exercise 8.2 Juggling with Schema and Mode Mindfulness in Personal Interactions[6]

Being-mode

- Grab a ball and stand about two meters across from another participant, who also has a ball. Keep your back straight, make eye contact, and become mindful of your breath. If any thoughts or distractions draw you away from your breath, take note of this, compliment yourself for your alertness, and softly return to mindful breathing.
- Gradually expand your awareness to the rest of your body. Sense your feet touching the floor, your hand holding the ball, and the full physical experience of your body. If you notice yourself getting sidetracked, acknowledge that it is good to notice this, and then use the breath as a stepping stone back to physical awareness. After two minutes or so,

[6] This exercise is not included on the audio files

toss the ball in a low arc toward your partner. Your partner will throw it back in the same way. Continue to mindfully pass the ball back and forth. Observe one another's skills and slip-ups. Someone misses a ball, the balls collide midair, or one person throws a little harder than the other. Pay attention to which schemas and modes get triggered when this happens, while continuing to juggle. If you notice your attention slipping, or if you get caught up in your schemas and modes, appreciate your mindfulness of that distraction. If necessary, you can go back to your starting position by focusing on your breath, becoming aware of your body, and resuming the juggling exercise with renewed mindfulness. Practice with the balls for about five minutes.

Doing-mode

(Participants remain standing in place)

After completing this exercise, ask yourself some questions about your observations, your experiences while juggling. Closing your eyes, or softly gazing into space, may help you come up with answers.

- Where is your breath most strongly felt? Does it change in rate, depth, or location in the body? What else do you notice?
- What is happening in your body? Where are the strongest sensations taking place? What kind of emotions come up? For instance, the Unrelenting Standards/Hypocritical schema, or Demanding Parent mode, can lead you to judge your partner as clumsy, or to expect their performance level to match yours. The Insufficient Self-Control/Self-Discipline schema and the Impulsive Child can lead you to start throwing the ball faster and faster.

Follow-up sessions

There will be two follow-up sessions. The first follow-up meeting will take place in one month's time, with the second session scheduled two months later. Follow-up meetings are shorter than regular sessions and will last only one hour. Rather than imparting new techniques, the second follow-up session will focus on maintaining and developing previously learned skills, and will include evaluations. Time to discuss specific events or concerns within the group will be limited.

Follow-up Session 1

Today is the first of two follow-up sessions. This session is somewhat different from the previous meetings. We will meet for just one hour, which participants will use to reflect on their schema and mode mindfulness over the past month. We will address the following types of questions: In what ways have you been using the mindfulness exercises to become more aware of your schemas and modes? Which aspects of your practice have gone well thus far, and what has been more challenging? What do you plan to continue working on in the future? Have you considered how you will avoid falling back on the habit of reacting to schemas and modes on automatic pilot?

Continued development of a mindful orientation

You cannot expect your newly learned skills to work *automatically* after just eight training sessions. Consistent use of mindfulness skills in daily life requires extensive training and discipline. In this way it can be compared to playing a sport or an instrument. Stress or fatigue from the whirl of everyday life may lead you to put mindfulness on the back burner, allowing your habitual schema- and mode-based reactions to creep back; that is why we encourage you to keep practicing and developing these skills. You can view mindfulness

169

practice as a kind of medicine which needs to be applied daily. What is your prescription? Short exercises or longer meditations? An exercise from the book? One that concentrates on schemas and/or modes? One meant to raise awareness of other people's intentions? An exercise for cultivating mindfulness of the Healthy Adult? The time between the last training session and our first follow-up meeting can be used to contemplate which mindfulness exercises may benefit you most in the future.

The first follow-up session reveals that, over the past month, Kate has frequently reacted to situations in Impulsive Child mode. Though unaware of this pattern at the time, the follow-up session allows her to recognize her impulsiveness. There have been lots of exciting developments in Kate's life of late: She met some fascinating new people, and she has been put in charge of a new project in the office. Yet during the mindfulness exercise Kate realizes how little she has practiced being mindful. She also notices how irritable she is; this has become an important signal for her, indicating high levels of stress. When stressed, the tension in Kate's relationship with her partner escalates to terrible fights, sometimes leading to physical aggression. She uses the follow-up session as an opportunity to renew her intent to practice mindfulness at least three times a week. The exercises provide a reliable way for Kate to monitor her stress levels, schemas, and modes, which help her to avoid the Impulsive Child's automatic reactions.

During the follow-up session Susan expresses her wish for a mindfulness exercise designed specifically for her own schemas and modes. Such an exercise will help her to create a calm inner space from which she can nonjudgingly observe her thoughts, feelings, behavior, schemas, and modes. Being mindful of other people's schemas and modes, and their intentions in particular, is also helpful to Susan. It deepens her understanding of the fact that other people's actions are not always about her; that they may just be acting on their own schema triggers and modes. Realizing this has the added effect of invalidating Susan's Mistrust/Abuse schema. During the follow-up session the trainer provides Susan with a mindfulness exercise suited to her personal needs, schemas, and modes. It is not taken from the book, but has been tailored to Susan's situation. She records the exercise on her phone so she can listen to it at home.

Consider some potential strategies for staying on top of your mindfulness training in everyday life. Here are a few example strategies:

- Download a mindfulness app on your smartphone. This type of app allows you to set reminders that go off during the day, prompting you to spend a few minutes in mindfulness or practicing a specific exercise. Performing a search for "mindfulness" in the App Store or Google Play store will result in numerous useful apps to choose from.
- Use your smartphone's agenda to set scheduled practice times throughout your day. Consider using an alarm to remind you.
- Create a mindfulness exercise that is customized to your own particular needs. Your custom exercise may draw attention to any of the schemas and modes that play a role in your life. Determine the length of your exercise and the kind of language that suits your needs. You might want to ask someone to record the exercise on your phone, MP3 player, or laptop. Having a recording saved to your cell phone is particularly useful if you are often on the go.
- Choose a fixed moment in the week to pause and reflect on the following: (a) Mindfully consider which schemas and modes have arisen over the past week; (b) Have I practiced any mindfulness exercises? (c) If not, which factors may have kept me from doing so? (d) What kind of goals can I set for this coming week?

- Plan a weekly evaluation together with your partner or other significant person. It is often helpful to have someone there who can support your mindfulness endeavors.

Follow-up Session 1 Exercise

The Healthy Adult Who Brings Mindfulness to Daily Life

When you don't feel comfortable or when your head is full of worries, mindfulness training can be easily forgotten. This exercise is meant to help raise your awareness of the Healthy Adult, the mode that can bring mindfulness to the present moment throughout your daily activities.

Being-mode

- Sit down in a chair with an upright backrest. Keep your spine straight without leaning back.
- Allow your back to settle into a comfortable yet straight position.
- Rest your feet flatly on the floor.
- Close your eyes.
- Become mindful of your back. Sense the contact between your back and the chair. What do you feel? Now move your attention to your hands. Become mindful of the sensations in your hands. After this, move your attention to your feet. Take a few minutes to explore these sensations, just as you did in the Body Scan exercise.
- Become mindful of breathing; notice where you feel your breath happening right now. You might focus on the motion of your belly. Or on the air rushing in and out of your nose with every breath. Rest your attention wherever your breath feels most present.

Doing-mode

After resting in being-mode for a while, keep your eyes closed as you mindfully contemplate the following:

- Reflect on the past month with an open and curious mind. How has your Healthy Adult been mindful of your schemas and modes? Take some time to allow specific images and situations to come to mind, and do not judge them.
- The Healthy Adult monitors your sensitive triggers and sustains your mindfulness during exercises. If you have been inconsistent with your practice, you may notice the Punitive or Demanding Parent expressing criticism. Watch and see how—as the Healthy Adult—you are able to address yourself in a calm and friendly manner.
- If you have not practiced your mindfulness exercises, then the Healthy Adult can mindfully reflect on anything that may have hindered your practice. Did a particular schema or mode prevent you from creating the time or space for mindfulness? Whatever may be surfacing in this moment, simply allow it to arise, without judgment. If you find yourself losing focus, acknowledge your distraction and gently return to mindful contemplation.
- Now gradually return to your breath. Conscious of every breath going in and out, ask yourself what the Healthy Adult will need in the future to continue cultivating day-to-day mindfulness of your emotional experience. To be more present and aware. Thoughtfully consider what you can do to support your Healthy Adult in times to come.
- I will now slowly count to three, after which you may open your eyes. Before returning to doing-mode, spend a few moments being mindful of your presence and the world around you... 1... 2... 3.

Homework for Follow-up Session 2

- Read the text for Follow-up Session 1 and practice the mindfulness exercise, The Healthy Adult Who Brings Mindfulness to Daily Life
- Continue thinking of ways to support your mindfulness training on a daily basis. You can also use the suggestions mentioned in this text. Spend the coming month carrying out your plan(s) and strategies

Follow-up Session 2

Recently each of you met individually for an evaluation with one or both of the trainers. Today is our final meeting as a group. For some, the training received in this program will have adequately addressed your needs. Others will continue with their individual treatment plans. In today's session there will be an evaluation, along with a renewed focus on the future.

Training evaluation

Schemas and modes tend to make you perceive yourself, others, and the world in black and white. This occurs automatically and independent from your awareness. Without realizing it, the Failure schema might be running in the background, causing you to feel very insecure. This schema can lead you to believe that you haven't learned a thing from the Mindfulness and Schema Therapy training. In fact, participants regularly experience an increase in symptoms, schemas, and modes as the training ends. If this happens to you, do not be put off, as it is all part of the process. Even though the program is designed to help you become more mindful, you may actually notice a decrease in mindfulness as we approach the end of training. This may very well be a temporary side-effect; a personal reaction to the training coming to a close. Now is the time to be nonjudgmental, because it is precisely this kind of situation that can cause us to fall back on old habits and

174

the automatic pilot. Remember to be mindful of the influence of your schemas and modes as we meet to evaluate the training and our results.

> Danny is very critical of himself during the final follow-up session. The way he reacts to his partner—often coldly and bluntly—disturbs him. He can't stand her when she mopes and sulks about her problems, such as her failure to find a job. He knows she is doing her best, but he can't help feeling contempt when she gets "like that." He later manages to address his partner in Healthy Adult mode. He apologizes and explains how difficult it is for him to deal with her vulnerability—but that it's his problem, not hers. Danny's partner is visibly relieved that he can recognize his Punitive and Demanding Parent modes and the behavior they provoke.

Continued recognition and monitoring of your schemas and modes

The mindfulness exercises are a great tool to help you continue being mindful of your schemas and modes on a daily basis. However, it is very easy to fall back on the automatic patterns of your schemas and modes, and sticking to your mindfulness exercises can be a real challenge. Staying disciplined requires hard work and persistence.

Participants often wonder whether they should keep practicing mindfulness exercises after the training is over. Do they need to use the downloaded audio files every time they practice? In our experience, participants usually find ways to practice that suit their own needs. The best approach is to pick a strategy that fits with your lifestyle. That said, we recommend practicing regularly throughout the week. You can compare mindfulness training to physical exercise; hitting the gym once a month for an intensive workout is far less effective than two normal sessions per week. Furthermore, it gets easier the more it becomes a habit, so regular weekly practice tends to be far less challenging than the occasional exercise.

Listening to the exercise recordings is not a requirement. Many people end up memorizing their favorite exercises. Find out what works best for you. The goal is simply to be mindful, and there are many paths to achieving that goal. In the same vein, it is not necessary to spend a lot of time on exercises. Some people choose to rely on three-minute mindfulness exercises, as they can easily fit them into their day-to-day schedules. Regular, short exercises are just as effective as longer meditations.

Besides your schemas and modes, we also recommend reflecting on real-life situations in which you clearly demonstrated mindfulness. Recognizing and acknowledging such events can really boost your self-confidence. The same goes for experiences that work like anti-venom on your schemas and modes. Say you have used the past week to focus on your own inner experience (or that of others), and you come to realize that, in certain situations, you could have been a little more warm and understanding. This kind of mindful insight is effectively an anti-venom for your schemas and modes.

Plans for the future

In this final session we invite you to reflect on the strategies you came up with during our previous meeting. Which parts of your plan were you able to carry out? Which parts worked well, and which didn't? Without being judgmental, try to determine which strategies may have been ineffective. Is the mindfulness app on your phone a helpful tool? What came out of your plan to involve a significant other in your self-evaluation?

We recommend examining your strategy with a critical eye in order to decide what needs to be changed or fine-tuned for the future. Some people find it useful to write down their plans in a notebook. Others store them on their cell phones. Keep in mind that plans are never final, and strategies require frequent fine-tuning in order to keep them useful and up to date.

Session exercises

One of the two following exercises will be practiced during this session. The other exercise can be listened to at home.

The Healthy Adult Who Watches Over Your Vulnerability, Responds with Gentleness, and has Hope for the Future

This exercise will help you develop awareness of your Healthy Adult, the one who is mindful of your sensitivity, your vulnerability, and your core emotional needs. The Healthy Adult does not judge your inner experience, but simply allows it to occur.

Being-mode

- Sit down in a chair with an upright backrest. Keep your spine straight without leaning back.
- Allow your back to settle into a comfortable yet straight position.
- Rest your feet flatly on the floor.
- Close your eyes.
- Become mindful of your back. Sense the contact between your back and the chair. What do you feel? Now move your attention to your hands. Become mindful of the sensations in your hands. After this, move your attention to your feet. Take a few minutes to explore these sensations, just as you did in the Body Scan exercise.
- Become mindful of breathing; notice where you feel your breath happening right now. You might focus on the motion of your belly. Or on the air rushing in and out of your nose with every breath. Rest your attention wherever your breath feels most present.

Doing-mode

After resting in being-mode for a while, keep your eyes closed as you mindfully contemplate the following:

- Spend a while reflecting on the past week. Think of the times your sensitivity allowed your schemas to be triggered. Perhaps

177

you were moved or disturbed by a situation and painful or difficult emotions came up. Look back on these events without judgment; with a curious and open mind.

- If you notice your attention trailing off during this exercise, simply acknowledge the distraction and regain your focus. We are only human, and all of us get distracted.
- Consider whether the Healthy Adult was aware of your vulnerable modes during those difficult situations. See how mindful it was of the part of you that was hurt or struggled with painful emotions. Try to allow yourself to experience whatever your vulnerable mode may have thought and felt in those moments.
- The Healthy Adult does not judge your vulnerability; it approaches it gently and with softness. The Healthy Adult takes as much time as it needs to become mindful of your vulnerable modes. It seeks to provide all the space and care your vulnerability needs, both now and in the future.
- The Healthy Adult also takes your vulnerable mode's emotional needs into account. What did your vulnerable mode need during those situations last week? Did it seek another person's awareness or acknowledgment? A sense of its own boundaries? Some spontaneity? Anything else?
- If your Healthy Adult recognizes that your vulnerable mode does not understand its own needs, then the Healthy Adult remains nonjudgmental. It puts you at ease and watches out for any action-oriented reactions. It also inspires hope, by complimenting you on your mindfulness, and it reassures you that it takes time to learn how to identify your core emotional needs. That it's perfectly alright not to be an expert on this aspect of yourself. And that you have all the room you need, now and in the future, to mindfully work on learning about your emotional needs.
- Now gradually return to your breath. Conscious of every breath going in and out, ask yourself what the Healthy Adult

will need in the future to continue cultivating day-to-day mindfulness of your emotional experience. To be more present and aware. Thoughtfully consider what you can do to support your Healthy Adult in times to come.
- I will now slowly count to three, after which you may open your eyes. Before returning to doing-mode, spend a few moments being mindful of your presence and the world around you... 1... 2... 3.

Planning a Mindful Future

This exercise will help you to continue developing awareness of your Healthy Adult, who will support and watch over your mindfulness endeavors in the future—including the steps you will take to get there.

Being-mode

- Sit down in a chair with an upright backrest. Keep your spine straight without leaning back.
- Allow your back to settle into a comfortable yet straight position.
- Rest your feet flatly on the floor.
- Close your eyes.
- Become mindful of your back. Sense the contact between your back and the chair. What do you feel? Now move your attention to your hands. Become mindful of the sensations in your hands. After this, move your attention to your feet. Take a few minutes to explore these sensations, just as you did in the Body Scan exercise.
- Become mindful of breathing; notice where you feel your breath happening right now. You might focus on the motion

of your belly. Or on the air rushing in and out of your nose with every breath. Rest your attention wherever your breath feels most present.

Doing-mode

After resting in being-mode for a while, keep your eyes closed as you mindfully contemplate the following:

- Be mindful of the present moment, with openness and curiosity. Consider the plans you previously set in place to continue practicing mindfulness. Reflect on your plans without judging whether or not you carried them out.
- As you contemplate your plans, be mindful of any thoughts and emotions that may arise. Whatever comes up, just let it be; observe it without judging.
- As you reflect on your plans, do you notice a conscious desire to put them into action? Do you wish to make new plans for practicing mindfulness? Or do you prefer to just reflect, without jumping into doing-mode, and without feeling the urge to find an immediate solution?
- Now gradually return to your breath. Conscious of every breath going in and out, ask yourself what the Healthy Adult will need in the future to continue cultivating day-to-day mindfulness of your emotional experience. To be more present and aware. Thoughtfully consider what else your Healthy Adult may need to be more mindful in times to come.
- I will now slowly count to three, after which you may open your eyes. Before returning to doing-mode, spend a few moments being mindful of your presence and the world around you... 1... 2... 3.

This concludes our training program. We wish you lots of mindfulness in the future.

APPENDIX III-A

Homework Sheet

Everyday Mindfulness

An important step in developing schema and mode mindfulness is becoming aware, on a daily basis, of what is happening around you. One way to achieve this is by carrying out routine activities with greater awareness. Some people practice mindfully brushing their teeth, while others bring mindfulness to eating meals, washing dishes, or grocery shopping. Select a daily activity that is short and simple, which you would like to engage in with more presence and attention. Specific personal interactions that occur on a regular basis are also an opportunity for mindfulness. Approach such interactions with the same quality of attention and curiosity that you brought to the Raisin exercise. Mindfully observe all the experiences that present themselves during your chosen activity.

Some examples of simple daily activities:

* brushing your teeth
* getting (un)dressed
* putting in/removing your contact lenses
* blow-drying your hair
* applying your make-up
* drying off after a shower
* the first few bites of a meal
* going up a flight of stairs
* preparing and/or drinking a cup of coffee or tea
* listening to music

Mindfulness and Schema Therapy: A Practical Guide, First Edition.
Michiel van Vreeswijk, Jenny Broersen and Ger Schurink.
© 2014 John Wiley & Sons, Ltd. Published 2014 by John Wiley & Sons, Ltd.

- preparing (part of) a meal
- walking from your train/bus/subway station or parking spot to your destination
- (part of) a conversation over dinner with your spouse and/or children
- (part of) a daily telephone conversation with a parent.

These activities can be carried out at a normal tempo, or they can be slowed down to allow for greater mindfulness. Try to practice one activity for several consecutive days. Start each exercise by focusing on the most immediate aspect of the activity, such as the contact between the toothbrush and your teeth, gums, and tongue. Then gradually expand your attention to include other elements of your experience, such as your arm moving the toothbrush, other parts of your body, sights, sounds, smells, flavors, thoughts, and feelings.

APPENDIX III-B

Homework Sheet   Date: _____

Five-Facet M Questionnaire★

Please rate each of the following statements using the scale provided. Write the number in the blank that best describes <u>your own opinion</u> of what is <u>generally true for you</u>.

1	2	3	4	5
Never or very rarely true	Rarely true	Sometimes true	Often true	Very often or always true

_____ 1. When I'm walking, I deliberately notice the sensations of my body moving.

_____ 2. I'm good at finding words to describe my feelings.

_____ 3. I criticize myself for having irrational or inappropriate emotions.

_____ 4. I perceive my feelings and emotions without having to react to them.

_____ 5. When I do things, my mind wanders off and I'm easily distracted.

_____ 6. When I take a shower or bath, I stay alert to the sensations of water on my body.

★Reproduced with permission from Baer, R. A., Smith, T., Hopkins, J., Krietemeyer, J., & Toney, L. (2006). Using self-report assessment methods to explore facets of mindfulness. *Assessment, 13,* 27–45.

Mindfulness and Schema Therapy: A Practical Guide, First Edition.
Michiel van Vreeswijk, Jenny Broersen and Ger Schurink.
© 2014 John Wiley & Sons, Ltd. Published 2014 by John Wiley & Sons, Ltd.

_____ 7. I can easily put my beliefs, opinions, and expectations into words.

_____ 8. I don't pay attention to what I'm doing because I'm day-dreaming, worrying, or otherwise distracted.

_____ 9. I watch my feelings without getting lost in them.

_____ 10. I tell myself I shouldn't be feeling the way I'm feeling.

_____ 11. I notice how foods and drinks affect my thoughts, bodily sensations, and emotions.

_____ 12. It's hard for me to find the words to describe what I'm thinking.

_____ 13. I am easily distracted.

_____ 14. I believe some of my thoughts are abnormal or bad and I shouldn't think that way.

_____ 15. I pay attention to sensations, such as the wind in my hair or sun on my face.

_____ 16. I have trouble thinking of the right words to express how I feel about things.

_____ 17. I make judgments about whether my thoughts are good or bad.

_____ 18. I find it difficult to stay focused on what's happening in the present.

_____ 19. When I have distressing thoughts or images, I "step back" and am aware of the thought or image without getting taken over by it.

_____ 20. I pay attention to sounds, such as clocks ticking, birds chirping, or cars passing.

_____ 21. In difficult situations, I can pause without immediately reacting.

_____ 22. When I have a sensation in my body, it's difficult for me to describe it because I can't find the right words.

_____ 23. It seems I am "running on automatic" without much awareness of what I'm doing.

_____ 24. When I have distressing thoughts or images, I feel calm soon after.

_____ 25. I tell myself that I shouldn't be thinking the way I'm thinking.

_____ 26. I notice the smells and aromas of things.

_____ 27. Even when I'm feeling terribly upset, I can find a way to put it into words.

_____ 28. I rush through activities without being really attentive to them.

_____ 29. When I have distressing thoughts or images I am able just to notice them without reacting.

_____ 30. I think some of my emotions are bad or inappropriate and I shouldn't feel them.

_____ 31. I notice visual elements in art or nature, such as colors, shapes, textures, or patterns of light and shadow.

_____ 32. My natural tendency is to put my experiences into words.

_____ 33. When I have distressing thoughts or images, I just notice them and let them go.

_____ 34. I do jobs or tasks automatically without being aware of what I'm doing.

_____ 35. When I have distressing thoughts or images, I judge myself as good or bad, depending what the thought/image is about.

_____ 36. I pay attention to how my emotions affect my thoughts and behavior.

_____ 37. I can usually describe how I feel at the moment in considerable detail.

_____ 38. I find myself doing things without paying attention.

_____ 39. I disapprove of myself when I have irrational ideas.

APPENDIX III-C

Homework Sheet

Cultivating Schema Mindfulness

This form contains questions that will help you evaluate the strength of your schemas. Rate the degree to which you observed each schema on a weekly basis. It may help to reflect on your experiences: What kind of thoughts, feelings, behaviors, and physical sensations did you observe? How frequently did you notice each schema popping up? At what intensity? Did you experience any changes while being mindful of your schemas? Go through each of your three schemas in this way.

After filling in your score, use the last part of the sheet to write down whatever may have helped you to become more mindful of your schemas, schema modes, and schema behavior over the past week. If you know what helped you respond differently in a given situation, that is, with more schema and mode awareness (acting more in Healthy Adult or Happy Child mode), then we recommend writing that down as well.

1. Schema mindfulness score
    (fill in the schema below)

    _____

    Enter a mindfulness score reflecting the degree of mindfulness with which you observed the schema this week (0–10, where 0 represents no observation, and 10 represents exceptionally mindful observation).

Mindfulness and Schema Therapy: A Practical Guide, First Edition.
Michiel van Vreeswijk, Jenny Broersen and Ger Schurink.
© 2014 John Wiley & Sons, Ltd. Published 2014 by John Wiley & Sons, Ltd.

2. Schema mindfulness score
   (fill in the schema below)

   _____

   Enter a mindfulness score reflecting the degree of mindfulness with which you observed the schema this week (0–10, where 0 represents no observation, and 10 represents exceptionally mindful observation).

3. Schema mindfulness score
   (fill in the schema below)

   _____

   Enter a mindfulness score reflecting the degree of mindfulness with which you observed this schema this week (0–10, where 0 represents no observation, and 10 represents exceptionally mindful observation).

The following has/have helped me develop greater mindfulness of my schemas, schema modes, and schema behavior:

(consider altered ways of perceiving emotions, but also physical sensations and different ways of behaving)

_____

_____

_____

_____

187

APPENDIX III-D

Homework Sheet

Writing a Summary

Using your own words, write a short summary of the mindfulness session you just completed. Taking notes in your own words has been shown to be an effective method for enhancing memory. Use this form to record important ideas and other things you may have learned.

Number of sessions attended: ___
Number of sessions remaining: ___
Short summary of session   Date:_____

_____

_____

_____

What I would like to remember from this session:

_____

_____

_____

Homework:

1. Write a summary
2. Read up on the last session
3. Practice mindfulness

Improving schema and mode mindfulness requires regular practice. To assist this process we recommend keeping track of how frequently

Mindfulness and Schema Therapy: A Practical Guide, First Edition.
Michiel van Vreeswijk, Jenny Broersen and Ger Schurink.
© 2014 John Wiley & Sons, Ltd. Published 2014 by John Wiley & Sons, Ltd.

you practice specific exercises. In the following list, check off each item you have practiced at least four times this week (including the exercises that were assigned).

Practiced more than four times?
(If not, state the reason why. Doing so promotes mindful decision-making.)

Exercise 1.1: The Raisin Exercise
Exercise 2.1: Mindfulness of Your Environment
Exercise 3.1: Three Minute Breathing Space
Exercise 3.2: Mindfulness of Painful Memories
Exercise 3.3: Mindful Walking
Exercise 4.1: Mindful Juggling
Exercise 4.2: Cultivating Schema Mindfulness
Exercise 4.3: Getting to Know Your Schemas
Exercise 5.1: Three Minute Schema Mindfulness
Exercise 5.2: Mindful Acceptance of Self and Other
Exercise 6.1: Walking with Mindful Intent
Exercise 6.2: Letting Go of Schemas
Exercise 7.1: Mindfulness of the Healthy Adult and the Happy Child
Exercise 7.2: Preparing for the Future
Exercise 7.3: What Do the Healthy Adult and the Happy Child Need?
Exercise 7.4: Mindfulness of Schemas as Mere Thoughts
Exercise 8.1: Mindfulness of Yourself as Child and Adult
Exercise 8.2: Juggling with Schema and Mode Mindfulness in
              Personal Interactions

APPENDIX III-E

Schema Coping Questionnaire

Listed below are a number of statements that describe various (schema) behaviors. Read each statement carefully and evaluate to what extent it applies to you. Write a number between 1 and 6 next to each statement to indicate the score.

Scores:

1. Not at all applicable to me
2. Only slightly applicable to me
3. Moderately applicable to me
4. Significantly applicable to me
5. Highly applicable to me
6. Perfectly applicable to me

1. ____ I try to avoid feeling pain, sadness, or anger.
2. ____ I often get defensive when criticized by others.
3. ____ I frequently think to myself, 'I knew it...', or 'Just as I expected...'
4. ____ I typically work very hard, even when I'm running on empty.
5. ____ I prefer to do things on my own (without the assistance of others).
6. ____ I withdraw from others whenever I feel unhappy or angry.
7. ____ I believe I have good insight into the thoughts, feelings, and actions of others.
8. ____ I often experience physical symptoms while under stress.
9. ____ I regularly put the needs and desires of others above my own.
10. ____ I spend a lot of time analyzing how people react to me.

Mindfulness and Schema Therapy: A Practical Guide, First Edition.
Michiel van Vreeswijk, Jenny Broersen and Ger Schurink.
© 2014 John Wiley & Sons, Ltd. Published 2014 by John Wiley & Sons, Ltd.

11. ___ I watch a lot of TV or spend hours on the computer as a way to distract myself.
12. ___ I am very (self-) critical and constantly strive to have things running smoothly.
13. ___ I am convinced that everything I worry about will (sooner or later) come to pass.
14. ___ I often pretend to feel better than I actually I am.
15. ___ I am often disappointed by others.
16. ___ I normally go to sleep or seek distraction whenever I feel bad.

Scoring the schema coping strategies questionnaire: Items associated with each of the three schema-coping strategies are listed below. Average scores are calculated for each subscale. The frequency of fives and sixes in each subscale can also be counted. These figures indicate your dominant schema-coping strategy.

Schema avoidance
Items: 1, 6, 8, 11, 16

Schema overcompensation
Items: 2, 4, 5, 9, 12, 14

Schema surrender
Items: 3, 7, 10, 13, 15

Part IV
List of Audio Files

The following audio files can be found at
http://www.mfvanvreeswijk.com/

Bibliography

Aalderen, J. R. van, Donders, A. R. T., Spinhoven, P., Giommi, F., Barendregt, H. P., & Speckens, A. E. M. (2012). The efficacy of mindfulness-based cognitive therapy in recurrent depressed patients with and without a current depressive episode: A randomized controlled trial. *Psychological Medicine, 42*(5), 989–1001.

Arntz, A., Genderen, H. van, & Wijts, P. (2006). Persoonlijkheidsstoornissen. In W. Vandereycken, C. A. L. Hoogduin, & P. M. G. Emmelkamp (Eds.), *Handboek Psychopathologie deel 2, Klinische praktijk* (pp. 443–479). Houten: Bohn Stafleu van Loghum.

Arntz, A., & van Genderen, H. (2009). *Schema Therapy for Borderline Personality Disorder*. Oxford: Wiley-Blackwell.

Asselt, A. D. I. van, Dirksen, C. D., Arntz, A., Giesen-Bloo, J. H., Dyck, R. van, Spinhoven, P., Tilburg, W. van, Kremers, I. P., Nadort, M., & Severens, J. L. (2008). Outpatient psychotherapy for borderline personality disorder: Cost effectiveness of schema-focused therapy versus transference focused psychotherapy. *British Journal of Psychiatry, 192*, 450–457.

Bibliography

Atkinson, T. (2012). Schema Therapy for Couples: Healing Partners in a Relationship. In M. F. van Vreeswijk, J. Broersen, & M. Nadort, *The Wiley-Blackwell handbook of Schema Therapy, theory, research, and practice*. Oxford: Wiley-Blackwell.

Baer, R. A. (Ed.). (2010). *Assessing mindfulness and acceptance processes in clients: Illuminating the theory and practice of change*. Oakland: New Harbinger.

Baer, R. A., Smith, G. T., & Allen, K. B. (2004). Assessment of mindfulness by self-report: The Kentucky Inventory of Mindfulness Skills. *Assessment, 11*, 191–206.

Baer, R. A., Smith, T., Hopkins, J., Krietemeyer, J., & Toney, L. (2006). Using self-report assessment methods to explore facets of mindfulness. *Assessment, 13*, 27–45.

Baert, S., Goeleven, E., & Raedt, R. de (2006). Aandacht voor Mindfulness-Based Cognitive Therapy; en erna. *Gedragstherapie, 39*(1), 23–42.

Bamelis, L. M., Evers, S. M. A. A., Spinhoven, Ph., & Arntz, A. (2014). Results of a multicenter randomized controlled trial of the clinical effectiveness of Schema Therapy for personality disorders. *American Journal of Psychiatry, 171*, 305–322.

Barlow, D. H., Farchione, T. J., Fairholme, C. P., Ellard, K. K., Boisseau, C. L., Allen, L. B., & Ehrenreich- May, J. (2011). *Unified Protocol for Transdiagnostic Treatment of Emotional Disorders: Therapist guide*. New York: Oxford University Press.

Bernstein, D., Arntz, A., & Vos, M. E. de (2007). Schemagerichte therapie in forensische settings: theoretisch model en richtlijnen voor best clinical practice. *Tijdschrift voor Psychotherapie, 33*, 120–139.

Biegel, G. M., Brown, K. W., Shapiro, S. L., & Schubert, C. M. (2009). Mindfulness-based stress reduction for the treatment of adolescent psychiatric outpatients: A randomized clinical trial. *Journal of Consulting and Clinical Psychology, 77*(5), 855–866.

Bishop, S.R., Lau, M., Shapiro, S., Carlson, L., Anderson, N.D., Carmody, J., Segal, Z.V., et al. (2004). Mindfulness: A proposed operational definition. *Clinical Psychology: Science and Practice, 11*, 230–241.

Black, D. S. (2013). *Mindful research guide*. Retrieved from http://www.mindfulexperience.org/resources/trends_figure_cited.pdf.

Bowen, S., & Kurz, A. (2012). Between-session practice and therapeutic alliance as predictors of mindfulness after mindfulness-based relapse prevention. *Journal of Clinical Psychology, 68*, 236–245.

Bibliography

Brown, K. W., & Ryan, R. M. (2003). The benefits of being present: Mindfulness and its role in psychological well-being. *Journal of Personality and Social Psychology, 84*, 822–848.

Buchheld, N., Grossman, P., & Walach, H. (2011). Measuring mindfulness in insight meditation (vipassana) and meditation-based psychotherapy: The development of the Freiburg Mindfulness Inventory (FMI). *Journal for Meditation and Meditation Research, 1*, 11–34.

Carmody, J. (2009). Evolving conceptions of mindfulness in clinical settings. *Journal of Cognitive Psychotherapy, 23*, 270–280.

Carmody, J., & Baer, R. A. (2009). How long does a mindfulness-based stress reduction program need to be? A review of class contact hours and effect sizes for psychological distress. *Journal of Clinical Psychology, 65*(6), 627–638.

Carmody, J., Baer, R. A., Lykins, E. L .B., & Olendzki, N. (2009). An empirical study of the mechanisms of mindfulness in a mindfulness-based stress reduction program. *Journal of Clinical Psychology, 65*(6), 613–626.

Chadwick, P., Newman Taylor, K., & Abba, N. (2005). Mindfulness groups for people with psychosis. *Behavioural and Cognitive Psychotherapy, 33*, 351–359.

Chambers, R., Gullone, E., & Allen, N. B. (2009). Mindful emotion regulation: An integrative review. *Clinical Psychology Review, 29*, 560–572.

Chiesa, A., Calati, R., & Serretti, A. (2011). Does mindfulness training improve cognitive abilities? A systematic review of neuropsychological findings. *Clinical Psychology Review, 31*, 449–464.

Chiesa, A., Serretti, A. & Jakobsen, J. A. (2013). Mindfulness: Top-down or bottom-up emotion regulation strategy? *Clinical Psychology Review, 33*, 82–96.

Davidson, R. J., Kabat-Zinn, J., Schumacher, J., Rosenkrantz, M., Muller, D., Santorelli, S. F., Sheridan, J. F. (2003). Alterations in brain and immune function produced by mindfulness meditation. *Psychosomatic Medicine, 65*, 564–570.

Derogatis, L. R., & Spencer, P. M. (1982). *Administration and procedures: BSI. Manual I.* Baltimore, MD: Clinical Psychometric Research.

Farchione, T. J., Fairholme, C. P., Ellard, K. K., Boisseau, C. L., Thompson-Hollands, J., Carl, J. R., et al. (2012). Unified Protocol for Transdiagnostic Treatment of Emotional Disorders: A randomised controlled trial. *Behavior Therapy, 43*, 666–678.

197

Bibliography

Farrell, J., Shaw, I., & Webber, M. (2009). A schema-focused approach to group psychotherapy for outpatients with borderline personality disorder: A randomized controlled trial. *Journal of Behavior Therapy and Experimental Psychiatry, 40*, 317–328.

Fredrickson, B. L. (2004). The broaden and build theory of positive emotion. *Philosophical Transactions: Biological Sciences, 359*, 1367–1377.

Fulton, P. R. (2005). Mindfulness as clinical training. In C.K. Germer (Ed.), *Mindfulness and psychotherapy*. New York: Guilford Press.

Fulton, P. R. (2008). Anatta: Self, non-self and the therapist. In S. Hick & T. Bien (Eds.), *Mindfulness and therapeutic relationship*. New York: Guilford Press.

Förster, J., Friedman, R. S., Özelsel, A., & Denzler, M. (2006). Enactment of approach and avoidance behavior influences the scope of perceptual and conceptual attention. *Journal of Experimental Social Psychology, 42*, 133–146.

Förster, J., & Higgins, E. T. (2005). How global versus local perception fits regulatory focus. *Psychological Science, 16*, 631–636.

Geerdink, M. T., Jongman, E. J., & Scholing, H. A. (2012). Schema Therapy in Adolescents. In M.F. van Vreeswijk, J. Broersen, & M. Nadort. *The Wiley-Blackwell handbook of Schema Therapy, theory, research, and practice*. Oxford: Wiley-Blackwell.

Germer, C. K. (2005). *Mindfulness and psychotherapy*. New York: Guilford Press.

Geschwind, N., Peeters, F., Huibers, M., Os, J. van, & Wichers, M. (2012). Efficacy of mindfulness-based cognitive therapy in relation to prior history of depression: Randomised controlled trial. *British Journal of Psychiatry, 201*(4), 320–325.

Giesen-Bloo, J., Dyck, R. van, Spinhoven, P., Tilburg, W. van, Dirksen, C., Asselt, T. van, Kremers, I., Nadort, M., & Arntz, A. (2006). Outpatient psychotherapy for borderline personality disorder: A randomized trial of schema-focused therapy vs. transference-focused psychotherapy. *Archives of General Psychiatry, 63*, 649–658.

Goleman, D. (1988). *The meditative mind: The varieties of meditative experience*. New York: Tarcher/Putnam Books.

Grabovac, A. D., Lau, M. A., & Willet, B. R. (2011). Mechanisms of mindfulness: A Buddhist psychological model. *Mindfulness, 2*, 154–166.

Grepmair, L., Mitterlehner, F., Loew, T., Bachler, E., Rother, W., & Nickel, M. (2007). Promoting mindfulness in psychotherapists in training influences the treatment results of their patients: A randomized, double-blind, controlled study. *Psychotherapy and Psychosomatics, 76,* 332–338.

Gunaratana, B. H. (2011). *Mindfulness in plain English.* Sommervile:Wisdom.

Haeyen, S. (2006). Imaginatie in schemagerichte beeldende therapie. *Tijdschrift voor creatieve therapie,* 3–10.

Haeyen, S. (2007). *Niet uitleven maar beleven, beeldende therapie bij persoonlijkheidsproblematiek.* Houten: Bohn Stafleu van Loghum.

Hargus, E., Crane, C., Barnhofer, T., & Williams, J. M. (2010). Effects of mindfulness on meta-awareness and specificity of describing prodromal symptoms in suicidal depression. *Emotion, 10,* 34 – 42.

Hayes, S. C. (2005). Acceptance and commitment therapy, relational frame theory, and the third wave of behavioral and cognitive therapies. *Clinical Psychology and Psychotherapy, 11,* 137–144.

Hayes, S. C.,Wilson, K. G., Gifford, E. V., Follette, V. M., & Strosahl, K. (1996). Experiential avoidance and behavioral disorders: A functional dimensional approach to diagnosis and treatment. *Journal of Consulting and Clinical Psychology, 64,* 1152–1168.

Hill, C. L. & Updegraff, J. A. (2012). Mindfulness and its relationship to emotional regulation. *Emotion, 12*(1), 81–90.

Hofmann, S. G., Sawyer, A. T.,Witt, A. A., & Oh, D. (2010). The effect of mindfulness-based therapy on anxiety and depression: A meta-analytic review. *Journal of Consulting and Clinical Psychology, 78,* 169–183.

Hölzel, B. K., Carmody, J.,Vangel, M., Congleton, C.,Yerramsetti, S. M., Gard, T., & Lazar, S. W. (2011). Mindfulness practice leads to increases in regional brain gray matter density. *Psychiatry Research, 191,* 36–43.

Hout, M. A. van den, Engelhard, I. M., Beetsma, D., Slofstra, C., Hornsveld, H., & Houtveen, J. (2010). Commonalities, EMDR and MBCT: Eye movements and attentional breathing tax working memory and reduce vividness of aversive ideation. *Journal of Behavioral Therapy and Experimental Psychiatry, 42,* 423–431.

Jazaieri, H., Goldin, P. R., Werner, K., Ziv, M., & Gross, J. J. (2012). A randomized trial of MBSR versus aerobic exercise for social anxiety disorder. *Journal of Clinical Psychology, 68*(7), 715-731.

Kabat-Zinn, J. (1990). *Full catastrophe living: The program of the stress reduction clinic at the University of Massachusetts Medical Center.* New York: Delta.

Bibliography

Khoury, B., Lecomte, T., Fortin, G., Masse, M., Therien, P., Bouchard, C., & Hofmann, S. G. (2013). Mindfulness-based therapy: A comprehensive meta-analysis. *Clinical Psychological Review, 33*(6), 763–771.

Klainin-Yobas, P., Cho, M. A. A., & Creedy, D. (2012). Efficacy of mindfulness-based interventions on depressive symptoms among people with mental disorders: A meta-analysis. *International Journal of Nursing Studies, 49*(1), 109–121.

Klatt, M. D., Buckworth, J., & Malarkey, W. B. (2008). Effects of low-dose mindfulness-based stress reduction (MBSR-ld) on working adults. *Health Education and Behavior, 36*(3), 601–614.

Koster, E., Baert, S., & De Raedt, R. (2006). Aandachtstraining bij angst en depressie: een wetenschappelijke innovatie met klinische relevantie. *Gedragstherapie, 39*, 243–255.

Lambert, M. J., & Barley, D. E. (2001). Research summary on the therapeutic relationship and psychotherapy outcome. *Psychotherapy: Theory, Research, Practice, Training, 38*(4), 357–361.

Lambert, M. J., & Barley, D. E. (2002). Research summary on the therapeutic relationship and psychotherapy outcome. In J. C. Norcross (Ed.), *Psychotherapy relationships that work: Therapist contributions and responsiveness to patients.* New York: Oxford University Press.

Lobbestael, J., Vreeswijk, M. F. van, & Arntz, A. (2007). Shedding light on schema modes: A clarification of the mode concept and its current research status. *Netherlands Journal of Psychology, 63*, 76–85.

Lutz, A., Slagter, H. A., Dunne, J. D., & Davidson, R. J. (2008). Attention regulation and monitoring in meditation. *Trends in Cognitive Sciences, 12*, 163–169.

Ma, S. H., & Teasdale, J. D. (2004). Mindfulness-Based Cognitive Therapy for depression: Replication and exploration of differential relapse prevention effects. *Journal of Consulting and Clinical Psychology, 72*, 31–40.

McCabe, S. B., & Toman, P. E. (2000). Stimulus exposure duration in a deployment-of-attention task: Effects on dysphoric, recently dysphoric, and nondysphoric individuals. *Cognition and Emotion, 14*, 125–142.

McManus, F., Surawy, C., Muse, K., Vazquez-Montes, M., & Williams, J. M. (2012). A randomized clinical trial of mindfulness-based cognitive therapy versus unrestricted services for health anxiety (hypochondriasis). *Journal of Consulting and Clinical Psychology, 80*(5), 817–828.

Nadort, M., Dyck, R. van, Smit, J. H., Arntz, A., Spinhoven, P., Wensing, M., Giesen-Bloo, J., & Asselt, T. van (2009). Implementation of out-patient schema focused therapy for borderline personality disorder in general psychiatry.

Onraedt, T., Koster, E., Geraerts, E., Lissnyder, E. de, & Raedt, R. de (2011). *Werkgeheugen en depressie. De Psycholoog*, 14–24.

Perich, T., Manacavasgar, V., Mitchell, P., & Ball, J. (2013). The association between meditation practice and treatment outcome in Mindfulness-Based Cognitive Therapy for bipolar disorder. *Behaviour Research and Therapy, 51*(7), 338–343.

Piet, J., & Hougaard, E. (2011). The effect of mindfulness-based cognitive therapy for prevention of relapse in recurrent major depressive disorder: A systematic review and meta-analysis. *Clinical Psychology Review, 31*, 1032–1040.

Posner, M. I., & Petersen, S. E. (1990). The attention system of the human brain. *Annual Review of Neuroscience, 13*, 25–42.

Posner, M. I. & Rothbart, M. K. (1998). Attention, self-regulation and consciousness. *Philosophical Transactions of the Royal Society B, 353*, 1915–1927.

Rapgay, L., Bystritsky, A., Dafter, R. E., & Spearman, M. (2011). New strategies for combining mindfulness with integrative cognitive behavioral therapy for the treatment of generalized anxiety disorder. *Journal of Rational-Emotive & Cognitive Behavior Therapy, 29*(2), 92–119. doi: 10.1007/s10942-009-0095-z.

Rapgay, L. Ross, J. L., Petersen, O., Izquierdo, C., Harms, M., Hawa, S., & Couper, G. (2013). A proposed protocol integrating classical mindfulness with prolonged exposure therapy to treat posttraumatic stress disorder. *Mindfulness, 2*, 1–14.

Renner, F., Goor, M. van, Huibers, M., Arntz, A., Butz, B., & Bernstein, D. (2013). Short-term group schema cognitive-behavioral therapy for young adults with personality disorders and personality features: Associations with changes in symptomatic distress, schema, schema modes and coping styles. *Behaviour Research and Therapy, 51*, 487–492.

Rijkeboer, M. M., Genderen, H. van, & Arntz. A. (2007). Schemagerichte therapie. In E. H. M. Eurelings-Bontekoe, R. Verheul, & W. M. Snellen (Eds.), *Handboek persoonlijkheids-pathologie* (pp. 285–302). Houten: Bohn Stafleu van Loghum.

201

Bibliography

Schmidt, N. B., Joiner, T. E., Young, J. E., and Telch, M. J. (1995). The Schema Questionnaire: Investigation of psychometric properties and the hierarchical structure of a measure of maladaptive schema. *Cognitive Therapy and Research, 19,* 295–231.

Segal, Z. V., Williams, J. M. G., & Teasdale, J. D. (2002). *Mindfulness-Based Cognitive Therapy for depression.* New York: Guilford Press.

Segal, Z. V., Williams, J. M. G., & Teasdale, J. D. (2013). *Mindfulness-Based Cognitive Therapy for depression* (2nd ed.). New York: Guilford Press.

Siegle, G. J., Ghinassi, F., & Thase, M. E. (2007). Neurobehavioral therapies in the 21st century. Summary of an emerging field and an extended example of cognitive control training for depression. *Cognitive Therapy and Research, 31,* 235–262.

Simpson, S. G., Morrow, E., Vreeswijk, M. F. van, & Reid, C. (2010). Schema therapy for eating disorders: A pilot study. doi: 10.3389/fpsyg.2010.001.

Smalley, S. L., & Winston, D. (2010). *Fully present: The science, art, and practice of mindfulness.* Cambridge, UK: Da Capo.

Teasdale, J. D., Segal Z. V., & Williams, J. M. G. (1995). How does cognitive therapy prevent relapse and why should attentional control (mindfulness) training help? *Behaviour Research and Therapy, 33,* 225–239.

Teasdale, J. D., Segal, Z. V., Williams, J. M. G., Ridgeway, V. A., Soulsby, J. M., & Lau, M. A. (2000). Prevention of relapse/recurrence in major depression by Mindfulness-Based Cognitive Therapy. *Journal of Consulting and Clinical Psychology, 68,* 615–623.

Treanor, M. (2011). The potential impact of mindfulness as exposure and extinction learning in anxiety disorders. *Clinical Psychology Review, 4,* 617–675.

Vettese, L., Toneatto, T., Stea, J., Nguyen, L., & Wang, J. (2009). Do mindfulness meditation participants do their homework? And does it make a difference? A review of the empirical evidence. *Journal of Cognitive Psychotherapy, 23,* 198–225.

Vøllestad, J., Nielsen M. B., & Nielsen, G. H. (2012). Mindfulness- and acceptance-based interventions for anxiety disorders: A systematic review and meta-analysis. *British Journal of Clinical Psychology, 51*(3), 239–260.

Vreeswijk, M. F. van, Broersen, J., & Nadort, M. (2012). *The Wiley-Blackwell handbook of Schema Therapy, theory, research, and practice.* Oxford: Wiley-Blackwell.

Bibliography

Vreeswijk, M. F. van, Spinhoven, P., Eurlings-Bontekoe, E. H. M., & Broersen, J. (2012). Changes in symptom severity, schemas and modes in heterogeneous psychiatric patient groups following short-term schema cognitive-behavioural group therapy: A naturalistic pre-treatment and post-treatment design in an outpatient clinic. *Clinical Psychology & Psychotherapy*. doi: 10.1002/cpp.1813.

Wampold, B. E. (2001). *The great psychotherapy debate*. New York: Lawrence Erlbaum.

Watson, D. (2005). Rethinking the mood and anxiety disorders: A quantitative hierarchical model for DSM-V. *Journal of Abnormal Psychology, 114*, 522–536.

Williams, J. M. G., Teasdale, J. D., Segal, Z., & Kabat-Zinn, J. (2007). *Mindfulness en bevrijding van depressie*. Amsterdam: Uitgeverij Nieuwezijds.

Young, J. E., Klosko, J. S., & Weishaar, M. E. (2003). *Schema Therapy. A practitioner's guide*. New York: Guilford Press.

Young, J., Arntz, A., Atkinson, T., Lobbestael, J., Weishaar, M., Vreeswijk, M. F. van, & Klokman, J. (2007). *Schema Mode Inventory (SMI version 1)*. New York: Schema Therapy Institute.

Index

Mindfulness and Schema Therapy: A Practical Guide, First Edition.
Michiel van Vreeswijk, Jenny Broersen and Ger Schurink.
© 2014 John Wiley & Sons, Ltd. Published 2014 by John Wiley & Sons, Ltd.